IDIOMS WITH EXAMPLES AND PROVERBS

ALWAYS LEARNING SUCCESSFULLY
with ALS Books

LAWRENCE CHUI

Book Title: IDIOMS WITH EXAMPLES AND PROVERBS
ALWAYS LEARNING SUCCESSFULLY with **ALS** Books
Author: Lawrence Chui
First Printing: 2021
ISBN: 9798739327512

DEDICATION

I would like to express my heartfelt appreciation to my beloved mother for her valuable time in providing her suggestions to me about the font choice, front cover design, and interior book design.

I would also like to express my heartfelt appreciation to my beloved father for his valuable time in collaborating with me in the writing of the definitions for the idioms and proverbs and in the building of the examples for each of the Idioms.

I also would like to express my gratefulness to my dear parents for contributing their valuable time and working hard with me with the strenuous task of proofreading and finetuning all aspects of this reference guide.

Thank you very much again to both of my beloved parents for all of their continuous support and encouragement throughout my time of compiling this book.

Sincerely yours

Lawrence Chui

April 2021

TABLE OF CONTENTS

INTRODUCTION

English has a wealth of interesting idioms and proverbs worthy of learning and use.

It is of great importance for any speaker or learner of English to know some idioms and proverbs because they are used frequently and daily by people in verbal communication such as face-to-face, telephone, radio and television as well as in written communication such as documents, letters, and emails.

Listed alphabetically in the first and second section are 1,353 Idioms and 363 Proverbs respectively.

A full example is given for each idiom beside its definition to maximise your understanding as readers by demonstrating its correct usage. However, only definitions are provided for the proverbs.

Every effort has been made where possible in this reference guide to provide the clearest explanation of the meaning for each idiom and proverbs here, and I truly hope that this reference guide will assist you in understanding these.

Lawrence Chui

April 2021

IDIOMS WITH EXAMPLES

<table>
<tr><td>A</td></tr>
</table>

a bad apple ① It is someone whose actions, behaviour or words will have a bad influence on others, thereby causing trouble or creating problems for them. ▣ *Mary is a bad apple in our department because she frequently shows up late for work every morning.*

a bag of worms ① It is an extremely complicated situation that causes a lot of problems when someone begins to deal with it. ▣ *I originally thought that it was very simple to start a new research project from scratch but it was really a bag of worms during the first six months.*

a balancing act ① It is an action or a task performed in an attempt to successfully deal with two or more groups, people or situations that are in opposition with one another. ▣ *It is difficult for the UN to perform a balancing act between the two countries that are involved in a conflict.*

a baptism by fire ① It is a very difficult or unpleasant first experience of something, usually a new activity or job. ▣ *The purchasing manager delegated an important task of negotiating a purchase agreement with the clothes supplier to his assistant John. From John's perspective, the task was a baptism by fire.*

a baptism of fire ① It is a very difficult or unpleasant first experience of something, usually a new activity or job. ▣ *I was given a very large self-managed superannuation fund to manage last month, and this task was a baptism of fire.*

a battle of nerves ① (of two opposing groups of people) whereby they attempt to discourage each other by showing how clever or strong they are often before a competition or they try to frighten each other by making threats often before a battle ▣ *It was indeed a battle of nerves between the two sales teams as they competed to achieve the first place in the last month's net sales for the company.*

a big fish ① a powerful person or an important person ▣ *This gentleman is a big fish in our company.*

a bitter pill for someone to swallow ① It is a situation or fact, or an event that someone finds it difficult or unpleasant to accept. ▣

Accepting the tough water restrictions was a bitter pill for farmers to swallow.

a black mark   ① It is an expression of disapproval for something that someone has failed to do or someone has done wrong. ▣ *The supervisor gave his subordinate John a black mark in the annual performance evaluation report.*

a bleeding heart   ① It is someone who is excessively sympathetic towards the poor or the suffering people but does not provide any assistance to them in a practical way. ▣ *Although Richard is a bleeding heart, expressing his excessive sympathy for the very poor people in our country, he never takes any supportive actions to help them.*

a blessing in disguise   ① It is an event or a situation that unfortunately causes difficulties and problems at first, but unexpectedly brings advantages later. ▣ *It is really a blessing in disguise as ten staff from our department is scheduled to visit old people in nursing homes, but it does give us publicity in newspapers and magazines as well as help improve the company's image in the community.*

a blind alley   ① It is a method or situation that is neither effective nor fruitful. ▣ *My boss did not employ a replacement for a staff who had left the company and then changed the work procedures in order to save some money for the company, but I thought that sooner or later he would realise that it was a blind alley and that he needed to rethink about employing a replacement.*

a blind spot   ① It is something that someone does not know anything about or that someone does not have an understanding of, although someone feels that they should. ▣ *I am quite good at English but Mathematics is a blind spot as far as I am concerned.*

a body blow   ① It is something that causes great difficulty or disappointment to someone or a group. ▣ *The preliminary result of the election is a body blow to the Green Party.*

a bolt from the blue   ① It is an event or a piece of news that is unexpected and surprises someone completely. ▣ *A high achiever's failure in the final examination came as a bolt from the blue.*

a bolt out of the blue   ① It is an event or a piece of news that is unexpected and surprises someone completely. ▣ *Mary is a world champion for three years in succession but the fact that she has been beaten by the world No. 6 earlier today is a bolt out of the blue.*

a bone of contention ① It is used to describe an ongoing argument or discussion over an issue or a topic. ▣ *The annual increment of 2.5% in salary for junior staff members of the company is not a bone of contention.*

a breath of fresh air ① It is a person or something that is pleasantly different, new, and makes everything seem more exciting than what someone is used to. ▣ *My husband Richard has changed his bad habits and is now a breath of fresh air.*

a can of worms ① It is an extremely complicated situation that causes a lot of problems when someone begins to deal with it. ▣ *Every solution proposed by you to solve a problem will just open up a can of worms.*

a change of heart ① It is a time when someone changes their attitude, opinion, or plans. ▣ *She had a change of heart and decided to work for our company.*

a class act ① It is someone who performs exceptionally well at or is successful with what they do. ▣ *Rebecca is a class act in bowls.*

a clean bill of health ① It is a report on someone, which is given by a doctor, and this report states that someone is absolutely in good health and free of illness whatsoever. ▣ *Mary has been given a clean bill of health by her doctor after going through a series of medical checks.* ② It is a report on something, which is given by someone in authority, and this report states that something such as a building or machine is in a good or satisfactory condition, or is safe. ▣ *Of 100 models of the motor vehicles that were randomly selected for roadworthy inspection, only 80 were given a clean bill of health.*

a close call ① It is a situation in which something dangerous, undesirable, or unpleasant has almost happened to someone, but they manage to avoid it. ▣ *That was a close call. John succeeded in avoiding the overturning of his yacht in a severe storm yesterday.*

a cut above the rest ① (of someone or something) much better than other people or things of the same kind ▣ *In his last examination, my son had achieved the highest score in class and thought that he was a cut above the rest.*

a damp squib ① (of an event) a lot less exciting or impressive than expected ▣ *The dancing party last night proved to be a damp squib because half of the invitees did not turn up.*

a different kettle of fish ① It is used to mean that something differs from the one that someone has just mentioned. ▣ *Being familiar with grammar is one thing but being able to write a book is a different kettle of fish.*

a domino effect ① a situation in which one event, especially a bad one, causes several other similar ones to happen one after another ▣ *The plane has crashed into a mountainside killing all passengers on board. This accident is a domino effect.*

a drop in the ocean ① It is an amount of something so small or insignificant that it makes no real difference to a situation. ▣ *The government has introduced a congestion tax in this financial year. The amount raised from the tax will be used to build more roads to relieve congestion in the CBD, but it is indeed only a drop in the ocean.*

a false dawn ① a situation in which someone is misled by the hopeful sign that something good will happen but it does not happen at the end in a way that they would have expected ▣ *There were signs of economic recovery, but that was just a false dawn.*

a far cry from something ① very or completely different from something experienced or mentioned earlier ▣ *Living in the Central Business District is a far cry from living in the countryside.*

a fat cat ① It is someone who has a lot of money and power. ▣ *The CEO who recently has been given a very big increase in his annual salary is a fat cat in the company.*

a feeding frenzy ① It is an occasion in which a lot of people get involved in something, often in a negative, a destructive, or an uncontrollable way. ▣ *The movie put Canadian cinemagoers into a feeding frenzy.*

a fine line ① It is a point at which it is hard to tell the differences between two situations or activities, especially when one is acceptable and the other one is not. ▣ *There is a fine line between religion and superstition.*

a flash in the pan ① It is a sudden achievement or a success that quickly ends and is not likely to happen again or last. ▣ *This young singer has only one hit song from the start of his singing career. It is obvious that his success is just a flash in the pan.*

a flight of fancy ① It is an idea or plan that is pleasant to think about because it is full of imagination but lacks practicality. ▣ *This* *scientist is talking about a man going to Saturn, but this is just a flight of fancy at the present time.*

a free ride ① It is an advantage or opportunity that someone undeservedly gets without having done anything. ▣ *As Albert is son of the boss, he has got a free ride for his promotion to the position of manager.*

a game of cat and mouse ① It is a situation in which a person who intends to defeat another will try to find ways to confuse or deceive them. ▣ *Online dating is really a game of cat and mouse, as you will never know if the person exchanging messages with you on the internet is real.*

a game plan ① It is a plan for achieving a particular aim or success, especially in sports or business. ▣ *The school basketball team hopes to beat the team from another school in the next match so we have to come up with a game plan.*

a good bet ① It is used to mean that something is likely to be sensible, successful, suitable, or useful, or that something is likely to happen. ▣ *Comedy DVD movies are a good bet for birthday presents.*

a gravy train ① It is said to mean a way to make money without much effort, especially by having a job that is easy and well-paid ▣ *My sister ends up on a gravy train when she is married to this guy who owns one of the largest health food companies in this country.*

a grey area ① It is a situation or subject that nobody truly knows how to deal because it is complex and unclear. ▣ *I note that there is a grey area in the law regarding stolen animals.*

a guinea pig ① It is someone who is subjected to the testing of new ideas or methods. ▣ *John was the first person used as a guinea pig for the COVID-19 vaccine.*

a hard act to follow ① It is someone who is so good or successful at something that it is difficult for someone else coming after them to be as good. ▣ *He is a skilful chairman and will be a hard act to follow.*

a hidden agenda ① It is a secret purpose behind a plan or an activity, which is not made known to others. ▣ *The CEO denied that the recent company restructuring was part of a hidden agenda to downsize the workforce.*

a house of cards ① It is an organisation, a plan, or a system, which is usually a complicated one, that is very weak and can easily be destroyed or go wrong, or will probably collapse or fail. ▣ *My company has a stock re-ordering system but unfortunately it is a house of cards.*

a labour of love ① It is a difficult job or task that someone performs out of duty or purely for pleasure because they want to do it with no expectation of a large reward or payment for it. ▣ *John always repairs his car instead of letting a car repairer do this for him, and it is indeed a labour of love.*

a last-ditch attempt ① It is a final attempt to achieve something before it is too late to avoid disaster, even after a series of failed attempts. ▣ *John, a leader of the Labor Party, made a last-ditch attempt to save his party from electoral defeat so he resigned from his leadership.*

a last-ditch effort ① It is a final attempt to achieve something before it is too late to avoid disaster, even after a series of failed attempts. ▣ *Eventually, the two sides reached an agreement after their negotiators made a last-ditch effort to do so.*

a leading light ① It is someone who is important, successful, and active in an organisation or campaign. ▣ *John is a leading light in his campaign against climate change.*

a level playing field ① It is a situation that is fair because different people, companies, or countries compete on equal terms and each of them has the same chance of succeeding. ▣ *To ensure a level playing field, the government will introduce a new legislation to impose a 10% levy on any goods bought from overseas.*

a living hell ① It is a situation or place that is extremely unpleasant and makes someone suffer a lot. ▣ *Teaching disruptive students is a living hell for teachers.*

a long haul ① It is something that takes a great deal of effort and time to manage. ▣ *To get this classic car up and running is going to be a long haul given that I cannot source the spare parts for the car easily from the spare parts dealer.*

a loose cannon ① It is a person who behaves uncontrollably or unexpectedly in a way that is liable to cause problems for other people. ▣ *Helen is considered to be something of a loose cannon by her colleagues.*

a mixed bag ① It is an assortment of various ideas, people, or things. ▣ *People going to the dance parties that are organised by me every month are a mixed bag these days.*

a nest egg ① It is a sum of money saved for a time when it might be needed unexpectedly. ▣ *I started investing in the stock market when I was very young because I wanted to build a nest egg for my retirement.*

a new lease of life ① (of someone) to become healthy, happy, or active after being ill, sad, or weak ▣ *I was given a new lease of life when the judge gave me probation instead of jail time.*

a one-man band ① It is someone who does the activity entirely by themself without requiring any assistance from anyone else. ▣ *The company that Lawrence began as a one-man band now has a global reputation and employs about 800 people.*

a pain in the neck ① It is someone or something that is very irritating. ▣ *Writing articles on dull topics is a pain in the neck.*

a pat on the back ① These are the congratulations, praises, or appreciation for someone who performs something well. ▣ *My boss gives me a pat on the back because I work overtime almost every day.*

a pen pusher ① It is someone who works in an office in contrast to blue-collar jobs, and their job is often uninteresting. ▣ *Having worked in the office for more than 10 years, he is now tired of being a pen pusher and decides to quit and start his own business instead.*

a piece of cake ① It is something that can be done very easily. ▣ *This English test should be a piece of cake for you.*

a piece of the action ① It is a role or share in an activity or event that someone wants because it is either a moneymaking or a successful one, or because it is either an exciting or an interesting one. ▣ *He needs to be quick to grab his ticket to see the spectacular circus show this year if he wants a piece of the action.*

a pot of gold ① It is great wealth or something excellent that someone tries or hopes to get in the future, but is very unlikely to get. ▣ *Winning the jackpot at the pokies is a pot of gold in the mind of a compulsive gambler.*

a question mark hangs over something ① It is used to say something that gives someone uncertainty or doubt. ▣ *In the eyes of the public, a question mark hangs over the safety of the COVID-19 vaccine.*

a race against time ① It is a situation in which someone has to accomplish a task fairly quickly because they have very little time available before the deadline. ▣ *It was a race against time to get all the actors and actresses rehearsed for the play.*

a red herring ① It is a piece of information, a suggestion, or an action that is not only irrelevant but often deliberately diverts people's attention away from the main problem or subject. ▣ *A criminal who deliberately plays cat and mouse with the police will leave clues at the crime scene but at least one of them is a red herring.*

a reign of terror ① It is a period during which the government or ruler kills many of their political opponents. ▣ *A dictator had begun a reign of terror on those who opposed his political ideologies.*

a rotten apple ① It is someone whose actions, behaviour or words will have a bad influence on others, thereby causing trouble or creating problems for them. ▣ *No company wants to hire a rotten apple.*

a rude awakening ① It is a situation in which someone is suddenly made aware of an unpleasant fact or truth about something. ▣ *Before the election day, John was very confident that he would win but he had a rude awakening on the election day.*

a rule of thumb ① It is a general rule about something that someone is confident about telling someone else because it is right in most cases. ▣ *As a rule of thumb, children this age should not spend more than three hours watching television.*

a saving grace ① It is a good feature or quality in something or someone that makes them acceptable or that makes them from being completely bad. ▣ *A saving grace of Peter is his honesty.*

a sea change ① It is a complete change in someone's behaviour or attitude. ▣ *My naughty son was very rude to me last year. However, there is a sea change in his behaviour this month.*

a shot in the arm ① It is encouragement and help at a time when someone needs it very much. ▣ *During the last recession, our company established a new clothing factory that gave the local economy a shot in the arm by employing 500 new workers.*

a shoulder to cry on ① It is a person who listens to someone's problem, gives them sympathy, and provides them with emotional support so that they are becoming less anxious and upset than before. ▣ *My boyfriend is always there for me when I need a shoulder to cry on.*

a slap in the face ① It is an action of someone that upsets or insults someone else. ▣ *The fact that this thief was not convicted of shoplifting in my grocery store by the judge was a slap in the face for me.*

a slice of the action ① It is a role or share in an activity or event that someone wants because it is either a moneymaking or a successful one, or because it is either an exciting or an interesting one. ▣ *I noticed that most of the recently listed IPO offerings on the Stock Exchange opened at a large premium over the issue price on the first day of trading so more and more investors, especially mum-and-dad investors, would want a slice of the action.*

a small fortune ① a large amount of money ▣ *John made a small fortune because he had been trading shares on the stock market for the past two years or so.*

a smoke-filled room ① It is a place where people in authority of power such as politicians meet to discuss matters and make agreements in secret rather than in a more democratic or open way. ▣ *Our political party has a smoke-filled room in central Sydney.*

a stick to beat someone with ① It is something such as a fact, a reason, or an argument that can be used by someone else to criticise or blame someone because they either disapprove of them or dislike them. ▣ *Owing to the low national literacy rates, the education minister now has a stick to beat the teachers with.*

a sticking point ① It is a point on which it becomes impossible to reach an agreement. ▣ *North Korea's refusal to give up nuclear weapons has long been a sticking point between it and the USA.*

a stone's throw from somewhere ① a short distance from one place to another place ▣ *The church is a stone's throw from my house so I go there every Sunday to worship God.*

a stumbling block ① It is a circumstance, difficulty, or problem that stops someone from achieving something. ▣ *To undertake research on the new vaccine for coronavirus with a lack of qualified staff in our Research and Development Department is a stumbling block.*

a talking shop ① It is a fruitless discussion at a conference or meeting. ▣ *My country considers the United Nations to be a talking shop at most meetings.*

a tall order ① It is a task that is either almost impossible or very difficult to accomplish. ▣ *John tries to beat his opponent at a tennis match but that is a tall order.*

a thick skin ① It is used for describing someone who has the ability to not become or feel upset by someone else's criticism or insults. ▣ *As* *a politician, you must have a thick skin as you need to learn to take some unkind remarks.*

a thin skin　① It is used for describing someone who lacks the ability to not become or feel upset by someone else's criticism or insults. ▣ *As Johnny has a thin skin, he is unsuitable to become a politician.*

a thorn in someone's side　① It is someone else or something that is the cause of annoyance, pain, or trouble to someone on many occasions. ▣ *The neighbour who lets his dog defecate on my lawn is a thorn in my side.*

a tower of strength　① It is a person who provides a great deal of assistance or support to someone whenever they have encountered difficulties in their life. ▣ *Jessica, who was a close friend of mine, was a tower of strength to me during my troubled times.*

a track record　① It is the reputation that a company, a person, or a product has, which is based upon on all their failures and successes in the past. ▣ *My uncle has established a track record of excellence as a story writer.*

a vicious circle　① An unpleasant situation is said to be continuing when one problem leads to another problem, which in turn, worsens the initial problem. ▣ *I was in a vicious circle when I was heavily in debt. I paid one credit card with another credit card until I finally became bankrupt.*

a wake-up call　① It is a shocking event that makes people realise the need to take action to change a dangerous or difficult situation. ▣ *The judge said that the jail sentence of 5 years was intended to send a wake-up call to the public that shoplifting would not be tolerated by the community.*

a war of nerves　① (of two opposing groups of people) whereby they attempt to discourage each other by showing how clever or strong they are often before a competition or they try to frighten each other by making threats often before a battle ▣ *The union has been fighting a war of nerves with the management over pay.*

a war of words　① a situation in which groups of people or two people argue or criticise each other over a particular issue that they disagree about for a long time ▣ *I had a war of words with the neighbours about who should pay for the erection of a fence.*

a weak link ① It is the weakest or the unreliable part of a system, which may lead to failure in the whole system. ▣ *Malcolm seldom comes for training every day so he is a weak link in our basketball team.*

a white elephant ① It is something considered to be both costly and useless. ▣ *When the cinema first opened ten years ago, it was widely regarded as a white elephant. However, more and more people are now watching plays at the cinema, and the cinema owner expects a full house nearly every night.*

across the board ① (of development or a policy) to apply equally to all the areas of business or people connected with it ▣ *The reduction in the rice subsidies by the government will affect the people across the board.*

act the part ① (of someone) to behave in the manner of one who normally behaves in a particular role ▣ *Now that Paul is poor, he certainly acts the part.* ② (of someone) to behave suitably for a particular job, occasion, position, role, or situation ▣ *If Ryan wants to leave a good impression on his manager, he must act the part by working hard all the time.*

add fuel to the fire ① (of something done or happened) to worsen a bad situation or a disagreement ▣ *The economy formally went into recession in the last quarter but the government's announcement of a reduction in rice subsidies would only add fuel to the fire.*

all at sea ① It is used to describe someone who is confused or baffled by a situation. ▣ *When our family arrived in Australia, we were all at sea about the taxation laws relating to the assets held overseas by taxpayers.*

all eyes are on someone ① It is used to say that that every person is watching someone and is waiting to see what will happen. ▣ *All eyes are on the education minister right now to see how she will respond to the problem of the poor literacy rates in this country.* ② It is used to say that every person is paying attention to a particular person. ▣ *All eyes were on Alan as he swam his last lap in the relay race.*

all eyes are on something ① It is used to say that that every person is watching something and is waiting to see what will happen. ▣ *All eyes are on the NASA SpaceX Falcon 9 rocket to see whether it will successfully launch into space today.* ② It is used to say that every person is paying attention to a particular event or situation. ▣ *All eyes were on the inaugural launch of the moon rocket yesterday.*

all hell breaks loose ① It is used to mean that people suddenly become very noisy or angry because there is a lot of arguing, fighting, or fuss. ▣ *His sister wakes him up as a result of his failure in the secondary school's entrance examination and all hell breaks loose.*

all of a sudden ① quickly and unexpectedly ▣ *The rain was pouring down all of a sudden.*

along the line ① in the future, especially at a later stage in a process or after a situation or an activity that has been going on for a while ▣ *Somewhere along the line boxes and boxes of electrical goods went missing from the warehouse.*

along the lines of something ① similar to something in type ▣ *He usually starts with basic questions along the lines of "How are you?" and "Have you eaten your breakfast?".*

an eye for an eye ① It is the action of inflicting harm on someone equivalent to the injury suffered at their hands. ▣ *The judge said that sentencing John for four years for attacking his nephew with a broken glass would serve as a warning to the public not to revenge in the form of an eye for an eye.*

an eye for an eye and a tooth for a tooth ① It is the action of inflicting harm on someone equivalent to the injury suffered at their hands. ▣ *Although Richard was attacked by his cousin with a broken glass because of a woman with whom both of them were pursuing, his mother advised him not to revenge in the form of an eye for an eye and a tooth for a tooth and told him to report the matter to the police instead.*

an old chestnut ① It is an idea, a joke, a story, a statement, or a subject that has been discussed or repeated to such an extent that it is no longer of interest to the hearer. ▣ *Richardson always jokes about money but this is an old chestnut.*

an old flame ① It is someone with whom someone else used to have a romantic relationship. ▣ *Mary was an old flame of mine. I now have a new girlfriend called Susan.*

an old hand ① It is someone who has a great deal of experience of something because they have been doing it for a long time. ▣ *The plumber is an old hand because he has at least 30 years of experience in plumbing.*

an old wives' tale ① It is a commonly held belief based on traditional ideas, which is often inaccurate or incorrect because someone has proven it as being the case. ▣ *I don't know whether it is only an old wives' tale to feed a cold and starve a fever.*

an own goal ① a detriment to someone's own interest because of a failure at achieving something ▣ *My marketing staff failed to achieve sales target last month and this became an own goal for our marketing department.*

an unknown quantity ① It is a thing or person about which someone almost knows nothing. ▣ *I have been her boyfriend for over 7 years, but he is still very much an unknown quantity.*

another nail in the coffin ① It is one of a series of bad things that is a contributing factor in the failure of something or someone. ▣ *I am afraid that our workers' strike will be another nail in the coffin of the company.*

around the clock ① all day and all night with stopping ▣ *I have been working around the clock to finish the financial performance report in time for the Board Meeting to be held later this morning.*

as fit as a fiddle ① (of someone) very healthy and strong ▣ *Both of my parents are over 70 years old, but they are as fit as a fiddle.*

as long as your arm ① very long ▣ *You must have a list of tasks to complete as long as your arm.*

at a loss for words ① (of someone) to be unable to speak because they are in great shock, in amazement, full of admiration, etc. ▣ *I was at a loss for words when I had heard the bad news about the death of my uncle.*

at a low ebb ① in a bad or poor condition or state ▣ *He is at a low ebb after suffering from horrific injuries.*

at a pinch ① if absolutely essential ▣ *Five or more people could be arranged to sit together comfortably in one table to watch the fashion show at a pinch.*

at a price ① (of someone) involving someone else to accept something unpleasant before someone will give someone else something in return ▣ *Don't rely on him to provide you with any assistance because he will only help you at a price.* ② (of something) very expensive ▣ *You can buy high-quality Wagyu beef from your local butchers, but at a price.*

at a snail's pace ① extremely slowly ▣ *Despite the fact that the economy went out of recession in the last quarter of this year, the employment grew at a snail's pace.*

at any price ① whatever the cost and the difficulties may be ▣ *He is determined to succeed in his new project at any price.*

at every turn ① (of something that happens) continuously or very frequently, and usually prevents someone from doing what they want to do ▣ *I ask her to give me an opportunity to pursue her but she declines at every turn.*

at first glance ① when someone first finds out, looks at, or thinks about something ▣ *At first glance, her tip for making fluffy scrambled eggs seems practical.*

at first sight ① It is someone's first impression of someone else or something. ▣ *When I met my wife about ten years ago, it was love at first sight.* ② when someone first finds out, looks at, or thinks about something ▣ *At first sight, his tip for cleaning an electric cooker seems useful.*

at long last ① after a long time ▣ *At long last my demands have been met.*

at sea ① It is used to describe someone who is confused or baffled by a situation. ▣ *I was completely at sea with the new notes and coins that came into circulation earlier this morning.*

at someone's heels ① (of a person) following closely behind someone ▣ *There is a strange-looking man at your heels.*

at the behest of someone ① If something is done at the behest of someone, it is done at the request of someone or by order of someone. ▣ *Any bill that has been successfully passed through the two British houses of Parliament can be vetoed at the behest of the Queen if she does not agree with it.*

at the cutting edge of something ① at the forefront of technological advancement in a particular type of activity ▣ *This is a company that is at the cutting edge of mobile communications technology.*

at the drop of a hat ① immediately without having to pause and consider about it ▣ *In the event that you need help, please do phone me at the drop of a hat so that I can come to you straight away.*

at the eleventh hour ① almost too late or at the last possible moment ▣ *It was fortunate that I arrived at the examination venue at the eleventh hour yesterday.*

at the hands of someone ① (of a suffering or something that is nasty or unpleasant) caused or done by someone ▣ *It is a major shock to the world to hear news of innocent people who have died at the hands of terrorists.*

at the push of a button ① very easily ▣ *The Australian Tax Office can extract a whole list of large taxpayers from its computer system at the push of a button.*

at the sharp end of something ① involved in the area of any activity in which someone will encounter the most negative aspects of it ▣ *These men and women, who know how to deal with different criminals, are at the sharp end of law enforcement.*

at the top of the tree ① with the most important status or rank in a career or profession ▣ *As far as her accounting career is concerned, she is currently at the top of the tree.*

B

bad blood ① It is the hatred between people due to arguments in the past. ▣ *The bad blood between the two neighbours had started since they had bitter disputes over who was responsible for the payment of the retaining walls.*

bang the drum for something ① (of someone) to give strong support to something in public ▣ *The Australia Trade Minister is banging the drum for the wine industry in the country.*

be a dab hand at something ① (of someone) to be very good at doing a particular activity ▣ *John was a dab hand at tennis and played for his country when he was young.*

be a dead ringer for someone ① (of someone else's voice or looks) sounds or looks exactly like someone ▣ *An ordinary guy from California is unusual in one respect because he is a dead ringer for the US Vice-President.*

be a dirty word ① to be a subject, a word, an expression, or an idea of which many people disapprove because it is either bad or immoral ▣

GST is a dirty word as far as small businesses and consumers are concerned.

be a double-edged sword ① (of something) to have both positive and negative aspects to it ▣ *The strong Australian dollar is a double-edged sword. It reduces the costs of imports for foods but it raises the costs of exports for cars and electronics manufacturers.*

be a law unto yourself ① (of you) to behave independently without regard for the law, rules, or traditional ways of doing things ▣ *You should not be a law unto yourself just because you are now unemployed as a result of the lockdown of the entire country that is imposed by the government to curb the spread of COVID-19 during the pandemic.*

be a millstone around your neck ① (of something) to be a problem or responsibility that you cannot avoid and finds it hard or impossible to deal with ▣ *As your parents, we wish that you had not taken out a $900,000 mortgage to purchase your house because your current financial situation obviously shows that paying off a mortgage is a millstone around your neck.*

be a safe bet ① It is used to say that something seems certain to happen or that something will certainly happen. ▣ *It is a safe bet that my boyfriend will attend my birthday party tonight.*

be a shadow of someone's former self ① It is used to mean that someone has less health, influence, strength, or vitality, than they used to have. ▣ *After a long illness, the male tennis player ended up being a shadow of his former self.*

be a sore point with someone ① (of something or a subject) to make someone feel upset, angry, or embarrassed ▣ *Johnny told Mary that he intended to pursue her but he was rejected outright. It was a sore point with him indeed.*

be ahead of the game ① (of someone) to know about the most recent developments in an activity more than other people who are also involved in it so that they are well prepared to handle all possible contingencies ▣ *We should always keep abreast of new technologies in every field where possible so as to be ahead of the game.*

be alive and kicking ① (of someone) to be very active, energetic, healthy, or popular ▣ *Although my grandfather is over 80 years old, he is alive and kicking nevertheless.*

be all go ① (of a place) to be full of activity or very busy ▣ *It was all go in the market town this morning.*

be as good as new ① (of something) to be in an excellent condition in that it looks completely new ▣ *The sofa is as good as new, and I am trying to sell it on the gumtree website for a good price.*

be as safe as houses ① to be very safe ▣ *A safe deposit box offered by the bank to store your valuables will be as safe as houses.*

be at a loss ① (of someone) to not know what to say or do in a particular situation ▣ *These men have some difficulties in learning the Chinese language and are at a loss to know where to seek help.*

be at death's door ① (of someone) to be so ill or sick that they are close to dying or have a high likelihood of dying ▣ *When I visited my friend Albert at the hospital, he was at death's door.*

be at each other's throats ① (of two groups or people) to be arguing or fighting angrily and continually ▣ *My two sons are at each other's throats about who to marry first.*

be at full stretch ① to be using everything such as resources and staff that is available at the time ▣ *This hospital is at full stretch because of staff shortages.*

be at loggerheads over something ① (of two groups or people) to disagree strongly about something ▣ *The two parties are at loggerheads over the terms of the agreement.*

be at odds with someone ① (of someone else) to disagree with someone about something ▣ *I am at odds with my wife about when and where to travel overseas.*

be at odds with something ① (of one thing) to be different or very different from another thing ▣ *The statement of the witness in the court was at odds with what the newspaperman had written.*

be at the end of your tether ① (of you) to run out of your patience or strength ▣ *You must be at the end of your tether after spending a few hours of gardening without taking any breaks.* ② (of you) to feel that you cannot deal with a bad, difficult, or upsetting situation any more ▣ *You must be at the end of your tether with these disruptive students.*

be at your wits' end ① (of you) to be very desperate and worried about something without knowing how to deal with it ▣ *You are at your*

be back to square one ① (of someone) to do something from the beginning again because they have completely failed in their previous attempt ▣ *The pilot project does not work at all so we are back to square one now.*

be beyond price ① to be extremely important or valuable ▣ *Spending quality time with my family is beyond price.*

be bitten by the ... bug ① (of someone) to become very enthusiastic about something ▣ *He is bitten by the travel bug so he set off for a working holiday in England.*

be bursting at the seams ① (of a room or building) to be completely full, especially with people ▣ *In recent months, a lot of the refugees were approved for residing in Australia. This building was bursting at the seams because there were no more rooms left to house additional refugees.*

be caught in the act ① (of someone) to be discovered committing a crime or doing something secret or wrong ▣ *These four men were caught in the act of digging up a buried grave.*

be caught on the hop ① (of someone) to not able to respond appropriately or quickly for something that has happened because they are not ready to do so ▣ *The Prime Minister of Romania was caught on the hop when the army of the neighbouring country entered his country by force in order to take control of it.*

be child's play ① It is an act or a task that can be done or accomplished with the greatest of ease. ▣ *He thought that the project delegated to him by his boss was child's play.*

be dead in the water ① (of something) to have failed and have a little chance of hope of becoming successful again in the future ▣ *His latest scheme was dead in the water so he was back to square one.*

be economical with the truth ① (of someone) to avoid telling the true facts of a situation, or to be lying about it ▣ *John is indeed an honest man, and it is unfair to say that he is economical with the truth of the matter.*

be for the chop ① It is an idiom for describing someone who is expected to lose their job. ▣ *It seems that some employees are for the chop due to the downsizing policy of the company.* ② It is an idiom for describing something that is going to be cancelled, closed, eliminated, ended, or stopped. ▣ *There are rumours that some of the television shows are for the chop due to poor TV ratings.*

be gagging for something ① (of someone) to be very keen to do or have something ▣ *Richard has passed a driving test to become a truck driver so he is now gagging for a truck.*

be given the boot ① (of someone) to be dismissed or fired from their job or position ▣ *After the 3-month probation period for the job, Mary was given the boot because her job performance was really not up to par.*

be given the green light ① (of a plan, a project, or an action) to have the permission given to someone else to carry out it by someone who is in charge or authority ▣ *His proposed project has been given the green light by the manager.*

be glad to see the back of someone ① (of someone else) to want someone to leave ▣ *His boss was glad to see the back of Jessica because her job performance during the 3-month probation period was below acceptable standards.*

be going down the drain ① to be being destroyed or to be getting worse, with not much hope of recovery ▣ *A lot of the small businesses are going down the drain one by one due to the bad economic policies of this government.*

be going down the pan ① to be being destroyed or to be getting worse, with not much hope of recovery ▣ *Because of the COVID-19 pandemic, many small businesses are going down the pan.*

be going down the tubes ① to be being destroyed or to be getting worse, with not much hope of recovery ▣ *Many small businesses are going down the tubes because the government has implemented lockdown of the whole country following the breakout of the COVID-19 pandemic.*

be going places ① (of someone) to be likely to become very successful because they possess a lot of talents or abilities and are able to demonstrate it if required ▣ *I will be going places with all my talents I have.*

be hanging over someone's head ① It is used for describing something that someone is worried about because it may cause something bad or unpleasant to happen to them in the future. ▣ *What is hanging over my head is that I have a medical examination tomorrow.*

be head and shoulders above someone ① (of a person) to be much better than other people ▣ *In a contest for the republican presidential nominee, Donald Trump is head and shoulders above all other nominees.*

be history ① (of all the things happening in the past) to be no longer exciting, interesting, significant, or relevant ▣ *Don't worry about this matter, and it is history.*

be home and dry ① (of a contest or other activity) to win or be successful in, or to ultimately gain success or victory with certainty ▣ *Although there are still four weeks before polling day, the democratic candidate is very hopeful that he can be home and dry.*

be in a tight corner ① (of someone) to be in a very dangerous or a very difficult situation that is hard to deal with or escape from ▣ *The government is in a tight corner on exchange rates.*

be in a tight spot ① (of someone) to be in a very dangerous or a very difficult situation that is hard to deal with or escape from ▣ *I was in a tight spot because of what he recently did to me about the matter.*

be in hot water ① (of someone) to be in a situation in which they have done something wrong and people become angry with them ▣ *The Trade Minister is in hot water when he has failed to disclose his business interests in several trading companies.*

be in line for something ① (of someone) to be likely to receive something, especially something good ▣ *Alan is in line for a huge pay rise.*

be in on the act ① (of someone) to take or win advantage of something that was started by someone else ▣ *The IT staff did all the hard work of creating the Excel macros and automating the spreadsheets, and now the staff in other departments want to be in on the act.* ② (of someone) to take part in something that was started by someone else ▣ *There are many new companies that want to be in on the act and provide the fastest broadband service on the NBN.*

be in the bag ① If something is in the bag, it means that someone has certainty that they will achieve or obtain it. ▣ *After winning two rounds in the tennis match, it seemed that victory was in the bag for Richard.*

be in the black ① (of someone or a company) to not owe any money to another organisation or person ▣ *Our company's financial position* *has improved from being in the red last year to being in the black this year.*

be in the dark about something ① (of someone) to not know anything about something ▣ *His daughter was in the dark about what had happened to my uncle who was later hospitalised.*

be in the driving seat ① (of someone) to have or take control of a situation ▣ *In politics, the conservative politicians of the Labor Party were in the driving seat, much to the desire of the moderates.*

be in the firing line ① (of someone) to be in a position or situation where they are likely to be blamed, attacked, or criticised ▣ *His parents were in the firing line because they deliberately allowed their children to behave very badly towards the mathematics teacher.*

be in the frame for something ① (of someone) to be thought to be responsible for an unpleasant situation or a crime, although this might not be true ▣ *Peter might be in the frame for the recent armed robberies.* ② (of someone) to be wanted by the police ▣ *They were in the frame for the terrorist attacks.* ③ (of someone) to have the chance to participate in something ▣ *Chelsea was in the frame for a place in the FA Cup Final 2020.* ④ (of someone) to participate in something ▣ *Albert is in the frame for the 2021 Wimbledon Championships.*

be in the loop ① (of someone) to be part of a group of people who make decisions about important things ▣ *A staff of five is responsible for interviewing and employing sales staff, and I am in the loop.*

be in the middle of doing something ① (of someone) to be busy with doing something ▣ *She is in the middle of sowing the carrot and lettuce seeds in her lovely vegetable garden.*

be in the middle of something ① (of someone) to be busy with doing something ▣ *Unfortunately, he is not available to take your call right now because he is in the middle of a staff meeting.*

be in the public eye ① (of someone) to be well-known and frequently written about in magazines and newspapers and often seen on television ▣ *Alan is a well-known funds manager who is in the public eye.*

be in the red ① (of someone or a company) to owe money to another organisation or person ▣ *I was in the red to my bank to the tune of one thousand dollars.*

be in the running for something ① (of someone or a country) to have a good chance or some hope of winning a competition or race ▣ *Let us guess which country is in the running for the 2021 ATP Tour.*

be in the same boat ① (of someone) to be in the same difficult or unpleasant situation as other people ▣ *My dad started going bald when he was in his fifties. 40 per cent of men over 50 years old are in the same boat.*

be in two minds about something ① (of someone) to be hesitant and be unable to decide about something ▣ *John is in two minds about pursuing Jane.*

be jumping up and down about something ① (of someone) to be very angry, excited, or upset about something ▣ *Mary is not someone who will be jumping up and down about unimportant things.*

be living on borrowed time ① (of someone) to continue to survive longer than expected, but usually for not much longer ▣ *Richard is living on borrowed time despite having got stomach cancer.*

be long on one thing and short on another ① to have very much of one thing but not very much of another thing ▣ *The Prime Minister's speech was long on words and short on practical action.*

be lost for words ① (of someone) to be unable to speak because they are in great shock, in amazement, full of admiration, etc. ▣ *I was lost for words because the singing performance was simply amazing.*

be lost on someone ① (of a joke said or a remark made by someone else) to be not noticed or understood by someone ▣ *My jokes were lost on most of my friends.*

be music to someone's ears ① (of a piece of information or news, or someone else's words) to be something that someone is very pleased to hear ▣ *The students in this class like their history teacher very much because her daily words of encouragement are music to their ears.*

be news to someone ① (of something) to be unaware by someone previously and they are surprised by it ▣ *Today is my girlfriend's birthday and that is news to me.*

be not a patch on something ① (of something else) to be much less attractive, good, etc. than something ▣ *The facilities of this public school are not a patch on those of the private schools, but the students think that they are very good.*

be not all it's cracked up to be ① (of something) to be not as good as people say it is ▣ *The bathroom facilities of this hotel are not all it's cracked up to be.*

be not everything it's cracked up to be ① (of something) to be not as good as people say it is ▣ *The recreation facilities provided in this park are not everything it's cracked up to be.*

be on a roll ① (of someone) to be very successful in what they are doing because they are making a lot of headway towards their job ▣ *Our football team has won five out of our six matches this season. We are on a roll.*

be on a slippery slope ① (of someone) to begin a course of action that cannot be easily stopped once it has started, which will inevitably lead to something disastrous, wrong, or unacceptable ▣ *He is on a slippery slope once he starts hanging out with the bad guys.*

be on course for something ① (of someone) to be likely to achieve something because they have already begun to do it or because they have already had some success ▣ *Shirley is on course for a tennis grand slam if she continues to play very well in each of her matches in the Australian Open.*

be on cloud nine ① (of someone) to be very happy ▣ *She was on cloud nine when she had found a new job.*

be on course to do something ① (of someone) to be likely to achieve something because they have already begun to do it or because they have already had some success ▣ *Rebecca is on course to win the World Championship in the women's figure skating.*

be on edge ① (of someone) to be in a state of instability, nervousness, or tension ▣ *I am on edge about going for a job interview this morning.*

be on someone's tail ① (of someone else) to follow someone closely, which often involves chasing them ▣ *John was on the thief's tail. He later caught him in the act, and finally handed him to the police.*

be on song ① (of someone) to be playing very well in a sports event ▣ *Our team played basketball with a team from another school yesterday and our whole team was on song.*

be on the cards ① (of something) to seem likely to happen ▣ *I think that an early presidential election is on the cards.*

be on the right track ① (of someone) to be doing something in a manner that is likely to result in success or bring good results ▣ *Our sales results have obviously shown that we are on the right track.*

be on the ropes ① (of someone) to be on the verge of collapse, defeat, or failure ▣ *The hotel developer is on the ropes because it is finding it increasingly difficult to remain within its budget.*

be on the same wavelength ① (of two people) to understand each other very well because they have the same interests, opinions, and attitudes ▣ *We can get along well with each other because we are on the same wavelength.*

be on the skids ① (of someone) to experience difficulties and not likely to continue successfully ▣ *The sole trader appears to be on the skids and is currently seeking financial assistance from the government.*

be on the spot ① (of someone) to be at the place where an event has recently happened or is happening ▣ *The police was on the spot within minutes.*

be on the wrong track ① (of someone) to be doing something in a manner that is likely to result in failure or lead to poor results ▣ *The poll has revealed that around half the voters believe our foreign minister is on the wrong track because other countries are starting to boycott our country's products.*

be on top of something ① (of someone) to be able to successfully control or deal with either a situation or a task, often a difficult one ▣ *We must strive to be on top of the new project.*

be on top of the world ① (of someone) to be extremely happy ▣ *I was on top of the world when each of my parents had bought me a very thoughtful birthday gift.*

be on your guard ① (of you) to pay attention to what is happening around you in order to avoid any possible forms of attack or danger ▣ *You should be on your guard against your enemies all the time because they are cruel and dangerous.*

be out of the frame for something ① (of someone) to be not thought to be responsible for an unpleasant situation or a crime, although this might not be true ▣ *The police say that they have found fresh evidence that proves that Alex is not the likely suspect and therefore he is out of the frame for arson.* ② (of someone) to be not wanted by the police ▣ *New witnesses of the recent home burglary came forward to the police and stated that Albert who was initially* *deemed as the suspect was not the one that they saw at the crime scene two days ago. As a result, the police confirmed that Albert was out of the frame for the recent home burglary.* ③ (of someone) to not have the chance to participate in something ▣ *Norwich City was out of the frame for a place in the FA Cup Semi-Final 2020.* ④ (of someone) to not participate in something ▣ *Unfortunately, one of the top Tennis players is out of the frame for the 2021 Wimbledon Championships due to personal injuries.*

be out of the question ① (of something) to be impossible ▣ *Agreeing to the outrageous contract demands is out of the question.* ② (of something) to be not allowed ▣ *Basically, a trip outside Australia is out of the question at the present moment due to a government ban on all overseas travel with the exception of New Zealand.*

be out of your depth ① (of you) to say that you do not have either any or enough experience, knowledge, or skills to deal with a particular situation or subject ▣ *I was out of my depth in my first job after my graduation from the University.*

be out of your mind ① (of you) to be stupid, crazy, or insane ▣ *You must be out of your mind paying several thousand for a box of cigars.*

be par for the course ① to be normally expected ▣ *For elderly people, sleeping for eight hours every day is par for the course.*

be plain sailing ① (of a job, a task, a test, or an activity) to be easy or simple, and free of difficulties, problems, or worries ▣ *I really had some difficulty in answering the first question of the test, but the rest of the questions were plain sailing.*

be poles apart ① (of two people or things) to be very different from each other ▣ *My friend and I are poles apart in taste when we buy our clothes.*

be pushing up the daisies ① (of someone) to be dead ▣ *If he continues to do daredevil stunts, he will probably be pushing up the daisies soon.*

be quick off the mark ① (of someone) to be quick to act in or react to an event or a situation ▣ *The price cuts on all sort of products during the festive season are good for bargain hunters who are quick off the mark.*

be riding high ① (of someone) to be very happy and confident, very popular or successful at present ▣ *The president-elect is riding high after winning the presidential election.*

be skating on thin ice ① (of someone) to be doing something that may get themself into trouble and that may end in unpleasant or severe consequences ▣ *He will be skating on thin ice if he gets caught drink-driving.*

be slow off the mark ① (of someone) to be slow to act in or react to an event or a situation ▣ *You will be at a disadvantage if you are slow off the mark trying to apply for a job vacancy.*

be streets ahead of someone ① (of someone else) to be much better than someone ▣ *Alan is streets ahead of his classmates at writing business correspondence.*

be streets ahead of something ① (of something else) to be much better than something ▣ *Alien technologies are streets ahead of our own technologies.*

be stuck in the groove ① (of someone) to become or feel bored because for a long time they have been doing either the same thing or something in the same manner ▣ *These white-collar workers were stuck in the groove in their jobs.*

be there for someone ① (of someone else) to be available to provide assistance and support for someone when needed or to make them feel better ▣ *I promised to be there for my friend Jenny after the death of her mother.*

be thin on the ground ① If people or things are thin on the ground, it means that there are not many of them. ▣ *Because more and more people buy books over the internet from online bookshops, traditional bookshops are thin on the ground these days.*

be thrown in at the deep end ① (of someone) to begin doing a job or task that is difficult and new without any preparation or assistance ▣ *John decided to be thrown in at the deep end to buy a poultry farm and learn to run the farm himself.*

be under fire ① (of someone) to be met with strong criticisms for what they have done ▣ *The president is under fire for his mishandling of the COVID-19 pandemic.*

be under someone's thumb ① (of someone else) to be completely controlled by someone ▣ *My friend told me that he was under his wife's thumb when it was related to spending money.*

be up in arms about something ① (of a group of people) to be very angry and be ready to complain or protest about something ▣

Residents are up in arms about a plan of the government to build a big dam near their homes.

be up in arms over something ① (of a group of people) to be very angry and be ready to complain or protest about something ▣ *The employees are up in arms over the poor annual salary increases.*

be up to your neck in something ① (of you) to be very busy with something ▣ *You must be up to your neck in work at the present moment.*

be up to your old tricks ① (of you) to be behaving dishonestly or foolishly, which is typical of your behaviour ▣ *You must the same man who is up to your old tricks again.*

be waited on hand and foot ① (of someone) to be looked after by another person who cares for them in every way and makes them comfortable ▣ *A hotel that offers you luxurious services will let you enjoy the ultimate experience of being waited on hand and foot.*

be your best bet ① used by someone when giving you their advice such as a course of action or their suggestion of something and indicating it to be your best choice or decision ▣ *If you want to get around Canberra in a convenient and cost-effective way, the public bus is your best bet.*

bear fruit ① (of something done by someone) to produce good results or to be successful, especially after a long period ▣ *If we expect to bear fruit in the future, we must work hard towards our goals.*

bear the brunt of something ① (of someone) to have endured the most mental or physical pain due to a predicament or problem ▣ *The bus driver bore the brunt of the impact when his bus collided with another vehicle.*

beat someone at their own game ① (of someone else) to beat someone or fight back against them in an activity, although they have a reputation for doing it very well ▣ *In the last match of tennis with me, my friend employed a new tactic and defeated me. However, I have beaten him at his own game in today's match.*

beat someone hands down ① (of someone else) to defeat someone with ease ▣ *Alan beat Albert hands down when they played Ping-Pong last week.*

beat your breast ① (of you) to make an exaggerated display of despair, sorrow, or regret ▣ *I think that you as a football coach are always thoughtful of your team players although another team has* *defeated yours in the last match. You do not beat your breast all the time as you know that more training is needed for your team to beat other teams in the future.*

beat your chest ① (of you) to make an exaggerated display of despair, sorrow, or regret ▣ *My friend thinks that you beat your chest after hearing the news about the death of your uncle.*

before you could say Jack Robinson ① It is used to mean that something happened very quickly or suddenly. ▣ *Our son went out of our house when the earthquake struck this country before you could say Jack Robinson.*

before your eyes ① If something happens before your eyes, it happens directly before you where you can see it clearly and you cannot do anything to change it or stop it. ▣ *The store manager spoke rudely to your mother and father before your eyes.*

beg the question ① (of someone) to make people want to pose a particular question that has not yet been answered ▣ *The actress is holding a press conference and she begs the question about her first love.*

behind the scenes ① secretly or privately ▣ *Let us applaud John and his three friends who worked behind the scenes to give us a great dance party tonight.*

behind the wheel ① (of someone) to be driving a motor vehicle ▣ *With the help of my binoculars, I would be able to see who is the good-looking guy behind the wheel.*

below par ① not up to the expected standard ▣ *Although the work performance in her present job is just below par, her boss still let her continue to work in this company after the 3-month probation period for a new staff.*

bend over backwards ① (of someone) to make a great deal of effort to do something that is good or helpful ▣ *I really appreciated my wife who bent over backwards to do everything at home to help me succeed as a politician.*

bend the rules ① (of someone) to change the rules, generally considered as neither harmful nor important, in the way of doing something that is not normally allowed, just either for giving an advantage to themself or for providing the help to another person ▣ *Students are not normally allowed to take an examination if they arrive* *late, but the teacher bends the rules this time after hearing this student's explanation.*

beyond someone's wildest dreams ① (of something achieved or happened) better than someone could have ever hoped for or imagined ▣ *Uncle Jack has achieved great success in his first business endeavours beyond his wildest dreams.*

beyond the pale ① completely not acceptable ▣ *Her boss has decided not to employ her after the three-month probation period because her work performance during the probation period is beyond the pale.*

bite the bullet ① (of someone) to force themself to do something difficult or unpleasant that they have been hesitating over or putting off ▣ *Alan is afraid to go to the dentist. He has no choice but to bite the bullet and visit the dentist because of the unbearable toothache.*

bite the dust ① to be defeated or destroyed ▣ *Many families bit the dust because one or more of their love ones had lost their lives due to COVID-19.* ② to die ▣ *Almost three million people around the world bit the dust due to the global pandemic of coronavirus disease 2019.* ③ to fail ▣ *Many businesses bit the dust during the COVID-19 Lockdown and these businesses had no choice but to close down.*

bite the hand that feeds you ① (of you) to not express thanks and misbehave towards someone who has helped or supported you ▣ *I personally think that you as the school principal should be very grateful of your sponsors who always donate drinks to the school's sports day held fortnightly, rather than biting the hand that feeds you.*

bite your tongue ① (of you) to refrain from saying a particular thing this time, even though you would really like to say it, because it is not the right time to do so ▣ *You had better bite your tongue if you want to keep your job.*

black and blue ① (of someone) badly bruised ▣ *Rebecca was black and blue after breaking up with her boyfriend.*

black-and-white ① (of a situation or subject) easy to understand what is right or wrong. ▣ *Retrenchment is not a black-and-white issue for the incumbent government.*

blaze a trail ① (of someone) to be the first to discover or do something important and new, which will facilitate others to do something similar in the future ▣ *The Labor Party is blazing a trail to recruit more women into its party so as to advance them into politics.*

bleed someone dry ① (of someone else, a country, or an organisation) to take a lot of money or resources from someone over a period of time ▣ *The University is bleeding my kids dry through high tertiary education fees.*

blood, sweat, and tears ① It is used to describe a project or task that is very hard to do and involves a great deal of effort or suffering. ▣ *The project to develop the coronavirus vaccine is not easy at all and involves blood, sweat, and tears of several scientists.*

blow someone's mind ① (of something that someone finds) to be extremely exciting, interesting, shocking, or surprising ▣ *I have received the news that will blow your mind and I think you will love it too.*

blow the whistle on someone ① (of someone else) to alert or tell the authorities about someone who is doing something bad ▣ *If you continue to come in late, I have no alternative but to blow the whistle on you and report this to the department head.*

blow up in your face ① (of a situation) to suddenly go wrong in such a way that it destroys your plan or your chances of something ▣ *I was surprised to hear that your plan to amaze your wife for her birthday blew up in your face when she thought that the gift you had bought was for another woman.*

blow your own trumpet ① (of you) to tell other people proudly about your own achievements in order to make them admire you ▣ *You still would not get the job, even if you blew your own trumpet in the job interview a few days ago.*

body and soul ① with all one's ability, effort, energy, or skills ▣ *A few scientists dedicated themselves to coronavirus research, body and soul.*

boiling point ① It is a situation that has become a very dangerous or worrying situation because the people involved are so upset that they are likely to go uncontrolled. ▣ *The situation in this country has reached boiling point, and the government can no longer tolerate this. Thus, it orders the army to keep it in order.*

break new ground ① to do something in an entirely different way ▣ *The coronavirus vaccine being developed by this company breaks new ground.*

break ranks ① (of someone) to flout the regulations or instructions of an organisation and voice their own opinion ▣ *The new police* *recruits who have just finished training for one year are warned that they must not break ranks.*

break someone's heart ① (of someone else) to make someone feel extremely sad and upset in that they put an end to a love affair or close relationship ▣ *He broke her heart when he ended the relationship with her.* ② (of a situation or an event) to make someone feel very sad or depressed ▣ *Knowing that more and more innocent lives are lost due to the global pandemic of coronavirus really does break my heart.*

break the bank ① (of something) to be too expensive ▣ *I will not waste my hard-earned cash on this laptop because it will break the bank.* ② (of something) to cost a lot of money ▣ *This blueberry muffin costs at least $8 and it will break the bank.*

break the ice ① (of someone) to say or do something to make people who have not met before feel more relaxed with each other at a meeting or party ▣ *When meeting Mary's parents for the first time to get approval for marrying their daughter, I felt very nervous. Her dad broke the ice by asking about my current job and everything went smoothly after that.*

break the mould of something ① (of someone) to do something completely in a new way rather than the traditional way ▣ *It is the stated ambition of the Prime Minister to break the mould of two-party politics and allow more political parties to form.*

bring someone to book ① (of someone else) to punish someone officially for what they have done wrong and make them explain for their actions ▣ *It is the right time to bring these shoplifters to book.*

bring someone to heel ① (of someone else) to force someone to obey them ▣ *At this age, you should not bring your children to heel. Just let them do what they want so long as what they want done is legal and reasonable.*

bring someone to its knees ① (of someone else) to defeat someone ▣ *The Romans soldiers brought their enemies to its knees.*

bring something home to someone ① (of someone else) to make someone fully realise to what extent something such as a situation, problem or danger is significant or very serious ▣ *I am living in this unit. I noticed some cracks in the concrete bricks in the frontage of the building recently so I brought this matter home to the Unit Management.*

bring something to a head ① (of a disagreement, a particular event or factor, a problem, or a situation) to reach a point where someone must deal with it without delay ▣ *I have been negotiating with the landlord about the reduction in rent for the apartment but unfortunately, we have so far not reached an agreement. It is about time that we need to bring the matter to a head.*

bring something to its knees ① (of an action or something else happened) to have such a bad effect on something that it cannot continue or function properly ▣ *The strikes brought the factory to its knees.*

bring the curtain down on something ① to cause or mark the end of something such as a situation or an event ▣ *My decision to retire early will bring the curtain down on my thirty-five years career in journalism.* ② to complete or finish something ▣ *The urgency to comply with the new accounting standards has forced the company to immediately bring the curtain down on the purchase and installation of the new accounting software.*

build bridges ① (of someone or a company) to help two countries, groups, or people who are in conflict with each other to develop a better relationship ▣ *The British Government looks for ways to build bridges between Mexico and United States.*

burn your boats ① (of you) to commit yourself irrevocably ▣ *If you work for the competitor after leaving your company, you will burn your boats.*

burn your bridges ① (of you) to commit yourself irrevocably ▣ *You really burned your bridges when you had tendered your resignation to your boss Peter before giving him a scolding in front of the whole staff.*

bury your head in the sand ① (of you) to deliberately ignore the truth about something unpleasant ▣ *This problem must be tackled head-on, and you should not bury your head in the sand.*

by leaps and bounds ① (of something that develops, grows, improves, or progresses) very quickly ▣ *His Chinese has improved by leaps and bounds this year.*

C

call a spade a spade ① (of someone) to directly and honestly say either what they think about something or what the truth is about something even if it is neither pleasant nor polite ◾ *Why don't you just call a spade a spade and say that your friend is a fibber?*

call it a day ① (of someone) to stop what they are doing because they either have done enough or do not wish to do any more ◾ *I have done more than four hours of gardening today. I decide to call it a day because I am feeling rather exhausted now.*

call someone names ① (of someone else) to use unpleasant words or expressions when they are talking to someone with a view to insulting or angering them ◾ *While I was in high school, some students called me names because I was too fat.*

call someone to heel ① (of someone else) to force someone to obey them ◾ *When your children are young, it is easier to call them to heel but when they grow older and older, it is difficult to do likewise as they no longer listen to you.*

call someone's bluff ① (of someone else) to tell someone to do what they are threatening to do to them because someone else believe that someone will not certainly do it ◾ *He threatened to harm me if I went out of my home, and I called his bluff.*

call the shots ① (of someone) to be in a position to control a situation and make all the informed and important decisions ◾ *In a war with the nearby country, the Defence Minister rather than the Prime Minister calls the shots.*

call the tune ① (of someone) to be in a position to control a situation and make all the informed and important decisions ◾ *He spends lots of money on his hobbies but does not allow his wife to buy clothes. He thinks that he has a right to call the tune as he is the only breadwinner.*

call time on something ① (of someone) to put a stop to something ◾ *The world tennis champion called time on his career because he had sustained severe leg injuries in a car accident.*

cannon fodder ① It is any of the combatants who is regarded or treated by the government or military command as expendable in the face of enemy fire. ◾ *The military officer told him that he was not allowed to refuse to be sent to the front lines as cannon fodder.*

can't take your eyes off someone ① (of you) to continue to look at someone because they are attractive ◾ *When you were first introduced to this young girl, she knew that you couldn't take your eyes off her.*

carrot and stick ① It is a way to induce someone to do something by offering them a reward if they do it well or by giving them a punishment if they do it poorly. ▣ *The congress intends to use a carrot and stick approach to entice the Democratic Party and the Republic Party to negotiate.*

carry the can ① (of someone) to take all the blame for something that they should not be the only person taking responsibility for ▣ *It was unfair for him to carry the can for a decision he did not make.*

carry the day ① (of someone) to be successful or victorious in a contest or debate against someone else ▣ *In a staff meeting where many attendees offered their ideas to solve one of the company's problems, the best one carried the day.*

carry weight ① (of someone's argument, opinion, etc.) to be respected and have much influence over other people ▣ *The health minister's argument in favour of the country's lockdown policy will carry weight in the Caucus Meeting.*

carve a niche ① (of someone) to become successful in getting the position or job that they want ▣ *Mary has carved a niche for herself as an ABC actor and her show attracts a regular audience of about 10 million. She is certain to be employed as long as the television network continues to broadcast the Television serials.*

carve out a niche ① (of someone) to become successful in getting the position or job that they want ▣ *John has carved out a niche for himself as an ABC newsreader and he is proud to have an audience of 15 million in his news programme in a week.*

cast a long shadow over something ① (of something) to have a negative as well as a lasting influence over something ▣ *Richard recently died of lung cancer due to smoking for a long time. This has casted a long shadow over all of his family members.*

cast a wide net ① (of someone) to consider or involve as many people or things as possible when they are doing something or looking for something ▣ *The computer manager has casted a wide net in his department in order to ascertain why the company-wide computer systems suddenly stopped working.*

cast caution to the wind ① (of someone) to act either rashly or recklessly ▣ *I cast caution to the wind by diving into the rough sea in an attempt to save the girl from drowning.*

cast your eye over something ① (of you) to examine, look at, or read something quickly ▣ *I noted that you were casting your eye over your bank statement that was received yesterday for any errors or omissions.*

catch someone off guard ① (of someone else's action or behaviour) to surprise someone by doing something unexpected for which they are unprepared ▣ *What catches me off guard is that I have got an invitation to her dance party, even though she knows that I am not a good dancer.*

catch someone red-handed ① (of someone else) to catch someone in the act of doing something illegal, sinful, or wrong ▣ *The police caught three robbers red-handed while they were robbing the bank.*

catch someone's eye ① (of someone else or something) to attract someone's attention because they are attractive or unusual enough to look at ▣ *That lady in the dance party has caught my eye.*

change hands ① (of something) to pass from one owner to another ▣ *How many times has this house changed hands in the last twenty years?*

change your tune ① (of you) to change your opinion completely about something, after knowing everything about it ▣ *You had insisted for many years that your uncle was dead long time ago. But recently, you changed your tune.*

cheek by jowl ① very close together ▣ *Mary has to live cheek by jowl with her aunt.*

chop and change ① (of someone) to keep changing their activities, ideas, jobs, mind, or plans ▣ *You cannot chop and change like this or else you will not be able to finish your project on time.*

clean up your act ① (of you) to improve your behaviour and begin acting in a more responsible and socially acceptable way ▣ *The Prime Minister warned you to clean up your act about your bad behaviour during the parliamentary meetings.*

clear the air ① (of someone or the government) to have a discussion with someone else over a problem in order to resolve it ▣ *The local government set up a committee of inquiry to look into the Policing Arrangements in order to clear the air.*

clear the decks ① (of someone) to do all the necessary or outstanding work first before getting ready to do other work ▣ *I must clear the decks before I consider other things.*

clip someone's wings ① (of someone else) to restrict the freedom of someone in what they want to do ▣ *I have been trying to clip my children's wings by giving them just enough money for their daily normal expenses.*

cloak-and-dagger ① It is used to describe an activity, an operation or a situation that involves espionage, intrigue, mystery, or secrecy. ▣ *Richardson worked as a spy for the American Government, and he was assigned to carry out a cloak-and-dagger operation in another country.*

close ranks ① (of someone) to completely support other members of a group or organisation and be against any outcomes or attacks from outside ▣ *All the cabinet ministers have closed ranks behind Prime Minister as far as the new legislation on child care support is concerned.*

come a cropper ① (of someone) to fail badly or completely, usually suddenly or unexpectedly ▣ *The sole trader who had brought a legal action against the newspaper for defamation of character came a cropper to win the lawsuit due to insufficient evidence.* ② (of someone) to suffer from a very bad fall ▣ *He came a cropper on the banked circular track while he was competing in this track cycling event.*

come clean with someone about something ① (of someone else) to tell someone the truth finally about something that they have been hiding ▣ *I hope that my son would come clean with me about attacking his younger brother over a financial dispute.*

come down to earth ① (of someone) to cease behaving or living in such a way that is impractical ▣ *John is not a kid any more and he should come down to earth by behaving like a proper adult.* ② (of someone) to start dealing with life and problems again after a period of great excitement ▣ *He will have to come down to earth after the long school holidays.*

come down to earth with a bump ① (of someone) to cease behaving or living in such a way that is impractical ▣ *Tina is not a teenager any more and she should come down to earth with a bump by living a proper lifestyle.* ② (of someone) to start dealing with life and problems again after a period of great excitement ▣ *When Alex goes back to work after his overseas trip, he will have to come down to earth with a bump.*

come face-to-face with someone ① (of someone else) to meet and talk to someone in person ▣ *In the criminal court, Mary came face-to-face with the rapist.*

come face-to-face with something ① (of someone) to be forced to face the reality of a situation or experience a problem, and have no choice but to accept or handle it ▣ *It was the first time that this patient came face-to-face with death but fortunately he survived this time.*

come full circle ① (of something such as an argument, an attitude, an idea, or a situation) to return to its original starting position after a long series of changes or events ▣ *Sooner or later, fashion comes full circle.*

come hard on the heels of something ① (of one event) to happen very soon after another event ▣ *The decision to buy my pullover came hard on the heels of an irresistible bargain in Amazon's website.*

come hell or high water ① (of something to be done) despite any difficulties, obstacles, or problems ▣ *I decided that I would get the project completed by the end of the month, come hell or high water.*

come home to roost ① (of someone) to have to deal with their own past mistakes that are the root of their problems ▣ *You should have known that your wrong action resulting from your wrong decision would come home to roost in the end.*

come hot on the heels of something ① (of one event) to happen very soon after another event ▣ *The new revelation comes hot on the heels of a previous press conference held some five months ago about the marriage of an actress.*

come in from the cold ① (of someone) to become accepted, active, or popular again after a period of lack of involvement or after falling out of popularity for some time ▣ *Over the last three years, the female singer has come in from the cold.*

come on stream ① (of something) to either be available for use or be in operation ▣ *My computer is in a bad state of repair. I need to get it repaired before it comes on stream.*

come out fighting ① (of someone) to do whatever it takes with a view to winning ▣ *The badminton player had lost 6 out of 10 matches in the last two years. She decided to come out fighting in order to up her performance in the next badminton match.*

come out of your shell ① (of you) to become less shy, more confident, more talkative, and more friendly ▣ *I think that you have come out of your shell now.*

come to a head ① (of a disagreement, a particular event or factor, a problem, or a situation) to reach a point where someone must deal with it without delay ▣ *The Australian Government's trade dispute with China has come to a head, and it is hoped that the dispute can be resolved by compromise.*

come to blows ① (of someone) to start a fight about something over which they show strong disagreement ▣ *Almost all the tenants of the units in this building come to blows over the landlord's decision to up rents by 20 per cent.*

come to light ① (of facts) to become known to people ▣ *New and irrefutable evidence has come to light that suggests she is definitely the one who has committed the recent brutal killings.*

come under fire ① (of someone) to be met with strong criticisms for what they have done ▣ *The Treasurer came under fire from critics and the public because he had included unusually large spending cuts in the next year's budget.*

come under the hammer ① (of something) to be offered for sale at an auction ▣ *This mansion will come under the hammer later today.*

come unstuck ① (of someone) to meet with difficulties and a failure ▣ *Yesterday, the football team defeated its competing team in the first round of the match but came unstuck in the second and third round. In other words, it was defeated by the competing team.*

come up trumps ① (of someone) to achieve a good result that is out of their expectation ▣ *Alan came up trumps, passing the hardest accountancy exam with flying colours.* ② (of someone) to assist someone else who has a problem to deal with by providing what is necessary to them, especially at the last moment and unexpectedly, so that they will succeed in solving it ▣ *At the last minute, Albert came up trumps by finding us an affordable hotel to stay while we were here for a holiday.* ③ (of someone) to do what is needed in order to make a particular situation successful, especially when this happens all of a sudden ▣ *Shirley came up trumps by providing me with plain flour, wholemeal flour, eggs, kefir, olive oil, and yeast so that I could make some bread for my family.*

come within a whisker of doing something ① (of someone) to almost succeed in doing something ▣ *Yesterday, the team of doctors came within a whisker of resuscitating their patient on the operating table.*

common-or-garden ① very ordinary ▣ *Whether John used a piece of specialised equipment or a common-or-garden bowl to combine the* *dry and wet ingredients, he still made a delicious loaf of home-made bread.*

cool your heels ① (of you) to feel bored or impatient because you have to wait somewhere without anything to do or someone forces you to wait ▣ *You must have cooled your heels because the Personnel Department from which you needed their information before your further work did not supply it to you in time.*

count the cost ① (of someone) to feel the adverse effects of an accident, a misjudgement, a mistake, etc. ▣ *Our home was completely gutted by fire last night. We are now counting the cost of not having taken out the home and contents insurance.*

cover your tracks ① (of you) to destroy or hide evidence of your actions or identity, because you wish to keep them secret ▣ *When you returned to the crime scene to cover your tracks, you should have realised that the police were going to have you arrested on the spot.*

cross someone's mind ① If something crosses someone's mind, they will think of it. ▣ *It never crossed my mind that Rebecca lied to me about the matter.*

cross someone's path ① (of someone else) to meet someone, usually unexpectedly ▣ *When I was invited to a dinner party, I crossed my sister's path.*

cross the line ① (of someone) to go beyond what is acceptable, for instance by participating in something anti-social or extreme ▣ *Although her cousin had been behaving badly in recent months, she did not think that she had crossed the line.*

cross your fingers ① (of you) to hope that something will happen in the way that you expected or wanted ▣ *The secondary school entrance examination for your son will take place at one o'clock in the afternoon. You should cross your fingers for him.*

cry wolf ① (of someone) to constantly ask for help when not needed or warn about danger when it does not really exist, so that people no longer believe them and will not help them when they really need help or are in real danger ▣ *After knowing the fact that her daughter cried wolf a number of times during a bushwalk yesterday, her parents advised her not to do it again otherwise nobody would come to her aid when she really needed help.*

cry your heart out ① (of you) to cry a lot and for a long time ▣ *When your boyfriend suddenly decided to end a long-term relationship with you, I could foresee that you were going to cry your heart out.*

cushion the blow ① (of a decision, a plan, or an action) to make something unpleasant seem less unpleasant ▣ *To cushion the blow of redundancy, the management decided to offer a generous severance package to each redundant staff.*

cut and dried ① (of a situation or solution) clear and unlikely to change ▣ *I do not consider the situation to be cut and dried as people think.*

cut corners ① (of someone) to do something in the cheapest, easiest, or quickest way, often by not following or ignoring the correct procedures or rules, or leaving something out ▣ *There is temptation for me to cut corners if you chase me up to complete the project two days ahead of schedule.*

cut loose from ① (of someone or something) to free themself or itself from the influences or control of someone else or something else ▣ *The British Parliament has voted to cut loose from the European Union after the yes vote from the referendum.*

cut someone down to size ① (of someone else) to show someone who is arrogant that they are not as clever, impressive, or important as they think they are ▣ *Although he thought that he had done an impressive work, I cut him down to size.*

cut something to the bone ① (of someone) to reduce something such as costs or resources to the lowest possible amount or level ▣ *Despite revising his original plan, he tried to break even by cutting costs to the bone.*

cut your losses ① (of you) to decide not to waste any more time, effort, energy, or money on an activity because it produces little or no result ▣ *Although you had made the wrong choice in buying these securities in the stock market, you did the right thing by selling them in order to cut your losses.*

cut your teeth doing something ① (of you) to get your first experience of doing something new, which will provide you with a foundation to do more complicated or advanced things later ▣ *You can cut your teeth working for The Australian Broadcasting Corporation, and have the chance of becoming a famous and a professional newsreader.*

cuts no ice with someone ① (of something) to have neither effect nor influence on someone ▣ *That sort of bad behaviour cuts no ice with the polite people.*

D

dead-end ① (of something) dull and not likely to lead to anything more successful or interesting ▣ *My first job after leaving University was a dead-end one, and I jumped ship after just one year with the company.*

deliver the goods ① (of someone) to accomplish something required or expected of them ▣ *I do not know whether the Prime Minister is in a position to stick to his election promises in the first year, but his supporters expect him to deliver the goods anyway.*

dig in your heels ① (of you) to refuse to change your mind in spite of other people's considerable and persuasive effort ▣ *Your staff find you unbearable because you dig in your heels and will not change your management style.*

dig into your pockets ① (of you) to use a lot of your own money to pay for or buy something ▣ *Are you going to dig into your pockets to throw a birthday party for your son?*

dig the dirt ① (of someone) to discover and reveal information about someone else that may cause damage to their reputation ▣ *The tabloid journalist digs the dirt about the unhappy marriage life of a famous actress.*

dig up dirt on someone ① (of someone else) to discover and reveal information about someone that may cause damage to their reputation ▣ *The Labor Party unlawfully hired a detective firm to dig up dirt on the Coalition Party leader who had been involved in the sex scandal.*

dig your heels in ① (of you) to refuse to change your mind in spite of other people's considerable and persuasive effort ▣ *You always dig your heels in what you believe to be morally right.*

dip into your pockets ① (of you) to use your own money to pay for something ▣ *I know that you have dipped into your pockets for your son-in-law's university fees.*

disappear into thin air ① (of someone) to disappear completely and suddenly ▣ *My sister-in-law disappeared into thin air for about ten years.*

divide and conquer ① It is a strategy, whereby you control others by making them argue with one another, adopted in a manner that allows you to stay in power because they are unable to oppose you. ▣ *The unions are concerned that the management may adopt a policy of divide and conquer to solve its wages dispute with the workers.*

divide and rule ① It is a strategy, whereby you control others by making them argue with one another, adopted in a manner that allows you to stay in power because they are unable to oppose you. ▣ *The management's strategy is simple: divide and rule.*

divide something down the middle ① (of someone or something) to either divide or separate something into two equal parts ▣ *Let's divide the lottery winnings down the middle.*

do a demolition job on someone ① (of someone else) to criticise someone's actions or ideas very strongly ▣ *Susan did a demolition job on Peter for his incompetent handling of the affair.*

do someone's dirty work ① (of someone else) to do something unpleasant, dishonest, or difficult for someone because they do not want to do it themself ▣ *The boss always delegated to his subordinates to do his dirty work.*

do something at one sitting ① (of someone) to do something from start to finish during one limited period of time ▣ *My son can easily eat a big packet of sweets at one sitting.*

do something at the touch of the button ① (of someone) to do something with great ease and speed, often with the help of technology ▣ *My company has specially trained several staff members to trace threatening calls at the touch of the button and to report the matter to the police.*

do something behind closed doors ① (of someone) to do something privately because there is a need to keep it secret ▣ *The cabinet discusses behind closed doors the need for the country to re-impose lockdown restrictions following the second wave of coronavirus.*

do something by the back door ① (of someone) to do something unofficially in secrecy hoping that other people do not realise what is happening ▣ *The government has taken protective and appropriate*

steps to disallow anyone including opposition leader as well as army to
sneak in by the back door and seize power by force.

do something by the book ① (of someone) to do something exactly in accordance with the regulations or rules ▣ *When the new police officers are on the beat for the first time, they have been instructed to be careful to do everything by the book.*

do something by the skin of your teeth ① (of you) to only just succeed in doing something ▣ *We all knew that the competitors were very competitive on the day of the golf tournament, and you were very lucky to have won the golf title by the skin of your teeth in 2009.*

do something in broad daylight ① (of someone) to do something illegal or morally unacceptable during the day when other people can see it and will find it unexpectedly shocking ▣ *Several armed men walked into the bank in broad daylight to grab more than $250,000 in cash from the tellers while some fifteen customers looked on.*

do something in one sitting ① (of someone) to do something from start to finish during one limited period of time ▣ *I sat down and read the whole book written by my son in one sitting.*

do something like a dream ① (of someone) to do something successfully or very well ▣ *This female singer performed at a concert last night and she sang like a dream.*

do something on the spot ① (of someone) to do something at once ▣ *You need to make a decision whether to buy the house on the spot.*

do something on the spur of the moment ① (of someone) to do something suddenly without any planning ▣ *In sentencing a criminal for his crime, the federal judges would make a decision after considering whether the killing was planned beforehand or the crime was committed on the spur of the moment.*

do something to the bitter end ① (of someone) to continue doing something in a determined way throughout until its completion ▣ *Due to the economic recession, the factory manager advised the workers earlier this week that the company was likely to go into liquidation if things did not improve, but the workers vowed to fight the closure to the bitter end.*

do the trick ① (of something) to have the wanted or necessary effect ▣ *If these self-help herbal therapies do not do the trick, then you should consult a family doctor.*

do your own thing ① (of you) to behave, do, or live in a manner that you want to without worrying about what anyone else thinks of you ▣ *Will your boss let you do your own thing when you report to him the progress in your project every day?*

down and out ① It is used to describe a person who is homeless, jobless, or penniless. ▣ *John knows best when it comes to helping a person who is down and out.*

down the line ① in the future, especially at a later stage in a process or after a situation or an activity that has been going on for a while ▣ *I think the situation will probably be a lot more different nine months down the line.*

down the road ① in the future, especially at a later stage in a process or after a situation or an activity that has been going on for a while ▣ *Don't worry about buying this computer. You can always upgrade it a bit further down the road.*

down the track ① in the future, especially at a later stage in a process or after a situation or an activity that has been going on for a while ▣ *No one will know what will happen to the company ten months down the track.*

down to earth ① (of someone) practical and realistic ▣ *If you want to achieve success in your project, you need to be down to earth about your own capabilities, limitations, and goals.*

down to the wire ① until the last possible moment ▣ *The US Congress needs to work down to the wire to reach a compromise on the budget by midnight today so as to avert the shutdown of all of the government departments because of insufficient funds.*

down-at-heel ① wearing old worn clothes because of poverty ▣ *Many companies went into liquidation recently and this resulted in a lot of homeless and down-at-heel people like Richard.*

drag your feet ① (of you) to take too much time to do something because you actually have no intention to do it ▣ *I note that you as the Minister of Environmental Affairs of the Republic of South Africa deliberately drag your feet on measures to deal with climate change. As a result, this provokes severe criticisms from other current world leaders.*

drag your heels ① (of you) to take too much time to do something because you actually have no intention to do it ▣ *If we don't set out* *now, we might be late for the dentist, so don't drag your heels and get into the car.*

draw a blank ① (of someone) to neither succeed in either finding the answer to a problem or finding the information, nor succeed in getting the results ◼ *The murder investigation has drawn a blank until now.*

draw the line at doing something ① (of someone) to accept or do something willingly but not beyond their limits ◼ *Susan doesn't mind wiping the dining table, but she draws the line at vacuuming the entire house.* ② (of someone) to not become involved or take part in a particular activity because they think it is very unacceptable and unreasonable to them, or it is wrong to them ◼ *Benjamin doesn't mind supporting you, but he draws the line at financing your campaign for equal rights.*

dress the part ① (of someone) to dress suitably for a particular job, occasion, position, role, or situation ◼ *If he wants to leave a good impression on the interviewer, he has got to dress the part.*

drive a coach and horses through something ① to break, destroy, weaken a claim, a plan, a rule, or an agreement, or render it ineffective ◼ *The recent findings drive a coach and horses through the claim that this company has been practicing eco-friendly activities.*

drive a wedge between people ① (of someone) to harm the good relationship between two people who are close ◼ *What John has told me about Mary appears to drive a wedge between her and me.*

drop a bombshell ① (of someone) to suddenly tell someone else an unexpected piece of bad news ◼ *My sister is on the phone. She drops a bombshell. She tells me that my girlfriend died of a heart attack yesterday.*

drop everything ① (of someone) to temporarily stop whatever they are currently doing in order to do something else more urgent ◼ *Maria dropped everything and rushed to the nearest dentist because she had got toothache.*

drop-dead gorgeous ① It is used to describe someone who is very attractive. ◼ *Maria is drop-dead gorgeous. That is why many young men want to pursue her.*

dyed-in-the-wool ① It is used to describe someone who has very strong beliefs or feelings about something and is not going to change their stance. ◼ *He is a dyed-in-the-wool traditionalist where internet is* *concerned. He prefers physical books to the internet when looking up for information.*

E

earn brownie points ① (of someone) to earn appreciation or approval for something favourable or good that they have done for someone else ▣ *I have earned brownie points from my wife for painting the driveway of our home.*

earn your spurs ① (of you) to have proven that you can do something well because you have already achieved something and that you can also be relied on to do something well in the future ▣ *Once you have taken care of the triplets for the entire day today after watching how one of the nurses has been caring for them in the hospital, you will earn your spurs as a caretaker.*

easier said than done ① It is used to mean that it is difficult to do something in practice that is theoretically simple to achieve. ▣ *You said that this project to provide an analysis of children's emotion was easy to complete but I thought that it was easier said than done.*

eat humble pie ① (of someone) to say that they made a mistake or did something wrong and feel sorry about it ▣ *You should eat humble pie for breaking my cup deliberately.*

eat like a horse ① (of someone) to eat a lot of food ▣ *Albert always eats like a horse but he is so thin nevertheless.*

eat someone out of house and home ① (of someone else) to eat a lot of someone's supply of food ▣ *We are worried that our friend Peter is going to eat us out of house and home because he will be staying at our house for a month or so.*

eat your heart out ① (of you) to draw the attention to yourself or someone else about something that you or they have achieved and at the same time mention the name of a famous person who does likewise just to make a joke that the famous person is not better than what you or they have done ▣ *Look at your great drawing! Eat your heart out, Pablo Picasso.*

eat your words ① (of you) to admit what was said by you before was wrong ▣ *You said that our basketball team would never win, but when our team will win tomorrow you will have to eat your words.*

every cloud has a silver lining ① There is something positive in any bad or unpleasant situation. ▣ *Every cloud has a silver lining. If I had not missed a train, I would never have met her and married her.*

F

face the music ① (of someone) to accept punishment or criticism for something that they have done wrong ▣ *It was I who had caused the project that our department was undertaking to be delayed. I and my boss had already faced the music because of this.*

fall by the wayside ① (of something) to be stopped making, using, or doing by the people ▣ *Jewellery falls by the wayside during a recession.* ② (of someone) to stop finishing a job or an activity ▣ *John told his girlfriend that he would make her a three-course meal tonight, but he fell by the wayside because he only made her the appetiser and the entrée, but not the dessert that she anticipated the most.*

fall flat ① (of an event or an endeavour to do something) to fail completely ▣ *His efforts to save his failing marriage fall flat.* ② (of a joke) to fail to amuse people ▣ *John cracks a lot of jokes in front of his girlfriend but none of them fall flat.*

fall foul of someone ① (of someone else) to get themself into trouble because they have failed to obey someone in authority or they have done something that makes someone angry ▣ *Please be careful not to fall foul of Adam because he is the bully in this high school.*

fall foul of something ① (of someone) to get themself into trouble because they have broken a guideline, a rule, or the law, or because they have done something wrong ▣ *I was worried about the homeless kids who will soon fall foul of the law.*

fall from grace ① (of someone) to stop being admired or liked by someone in authority because they have made a mistake, or they have done something wrong or immoral ▣ *Josephine fell from grace by her boss because she wrongly sold the company's goods to one customer at below cost, resulting in a loss of about $20,000 to the company.*

fall head over heels with someone ① (of someone else) to be completely or very much in love with someone, and often suddenly ▣ *Marian told her mother that she fell head over heels with Tommy.*

fall into place ① (of something that someone initially finds it complicated or difficult to understand, or that someone tries to understand) to suddenly become clear or organised in their mind, usually after they have pieced all the information together ▣ *When he studies the legal case again, all the particulars of the legal case fall into place.*

fall into someone's hands ① (of someone) to be captured by their opponent or enemy ▣ *The colonel fell into enemy's hands.* ② (of something) to become controlled by someone who is a dangerous enemy or person ▣ *When our soldiers retreated from the front line, some of our tanks fell into enemy's hands.* ③ (of something) to be taken by your opponent or enemy who could use it against you ▣ *When our soldiers retreated from the front line, all of our cannons fell into enemy's hands.*

fall into the trap of doing something ① (of someone) to get into a difficult situation or to make a mistake by either trusting someone else or doing something wrong ▣ *You should not fall into the trap of investing all your money into one stock.*

fall into the wrong hands ① (of someone) to be captured by their opponent or enemy ▣ *After the war, some 600 soldiers fell into the wrong hands as prisoners of war.* ② (of something) to become controlled by someone who is a dangerous enemy or person ▣ *There are fears that the weapons of the retreated soldiers could fall into the wrong hands.* ③ (of something) to be taken by your opponent or enemy who could use it against you ▣ *Some 200 soldiers considered that they were about to be surrounded by their enemies and they decided to retreat from the front line without their cannons and tanks, all of which could fall into the wrong hands.*

fall on deaf ears ① (of a suggestion or warning) to be ignored by someone ▣ *The boss told one of his subordinates to resign voluntarily because a big mistake in his daily work had led to a loss of about $50,000 to the company but his plea fell on deaf ears. Ultimately, the company had no alternative but to fire him.*

fall on your feet ① (of you) to get into a good situation not because you make an utmost effort yourself but because you are lucky ▣ *As a car salesman just for a few months, you really fell on your feet after receiving an order for 20 new cars from the company in one go.*

fall through the net ① If someone falls through the net, it means that a system has failed to deal with them as it is supposed to do. ▣ *With Australia's population approaching 26 million, it is easy for some* *people to fall through the net and not get vaccinated.* ② If someone or something falls through the net, it means that a system that was designed to check or assist them has failed to do this. ▣ *This group of people is responsible for looking for the homeless who have fallen through the net.*

fan the flames of something ① (of someone's action) to worsen a bad situation ▣ *His speeches will only serve to fan the flames of race riots.*

feel at home ① (of someone) to feel comfortable, happy, and relaxed in a particular place or situation ▣ *We have been feeling at home in our new apartment after moving into it a few weeks ago.*

feel hard done-by ① (of someone) to feel that they have not been treated fairly ▣ *One of my subordinates felt hard done-by and was not happy about it. He expressed his dissatisfaction with the head of the department.*

feel hard done-to ① (of someone) to feel that they have not been treated fairly ▣ *One of my work colleagues felt hard done-to and made a complaint to the department head.*

feel the pinch ① (of someone) to be in financial hardship, especially because they do not have as much money as they are used to have ▣ *Poor households will feel the pinch because of the imposition of 10% GST on all foods by the government.*

fight a losing battle ① (of someone) to try to achieve something when they are not very likely to succeed ▣ *Benjamin fought a losing battle against his prostate cancer.*

fight a rearguard action ① (of a company or someone) to try hard to prevent something from happening despite having little or no hope of success ▣ *The local retailers are fighting a rearguard action against competition from an international company that started operation in Australia just eight months ago.*

fight for your life ① (of you) to try very hard to stay alive because you are seriously ill or injured ▣ *If you were in a serious car accident, you would fight for your life.*

fight to the death to do something ① (of someone) to refuse giving up by either keeping hold of something or trying very hard to achieve something ▣ *I will fight to the death to win in the chess competition tomorrow - whatever it takes.*

fight your corner ① (of you) to defend what you believe about something strongly by arguing ▣ *Several regional managers supported you to undertake the project and said that you should fight your corner.*

find common ground ① (of two or more countries, groups, organisations, people, etc.) to reach an agreement on something ▣ *The participating countries appear to be unable to find common ground on the issues of climate change.*

fire a shot across someone's bows ① (of someone else) to do something in readiness for strong opposition against someone who does not change or stop ▣ *The Health Minister's own supporters are firing a shot across his bows.*

fire a warning shot across someone's bows ① (of someone else) to do something in readiness for strong opposition against someone who does not change or stop ▣ *The Prime Minister did not change his stance on abortion. His own supporters were firing a warning shot across his bows.*

firing on all cylinders ① (of someone, a group, or a team) performing at a peak level ▣ *The basketball team is firing on all cylinders.*

fit the bill ① (of someone) to be the right person as needed in a particular situation ▣ *John has more than ten years of teaching experience and he certainly fits the bill for filling the job vacancy.* ② (of something) to be the right thing as needed in a particular situation ▣ *This rectangular table will certainly fit the bill for hosting my first dinner party with my family and friends tonight.*

flavour of the month ① It is someone or something that is very popular at a particular time. ▣ *Josephine Cheung is undoubtedly the flavour of the month.*

flex your muscles ① (of you) to behave in a manner that is intended to exhibit your power or influence over others and that you have even considered using it ▣ *You have been doing your job more efficiently and much faster than other colleagues. It is now the time to flex your muscles and show the boss what you are capable of.*

fly in the face of something ① (of something else, usually an argument) to be totally against something such as ideas, practices, or rules accepted as norms ▣ *I am opposed to his views on the matter. His arguments seem to fly in the face of common sense.*

fly out the window ① (of someone's particular way of behaving or thinking, a plan, a quality, or an idea) to disappear entirely ▣ *After drinking one cup of water, all of my thirst flies out the window.*

fly the flag ① (of someone) to behave in a way to show their support for their country or a group to which they belong at a sporting event or a special occasion ▣ *Our Australian football team, which flew the flag, took second place in the 1976 Olympic Games.*

follow hard on the heels of something ① (of one event) to happen very soon after another event ▣ *The decision to sack one of my subordinates follows hard on the heels of his act of stealing the goods of the company.*

follow in someone's footsteps ① (of someone else) to do something in the same way as someone did ▣ *Alexander Wong is the son of a doctor and is a university student majoring in medicine. He wants to follow in his father's footsteps.*

follow something to the letter ① (of someone) to do something in accordance with the exact rules, regulations, instructions, or advice ▣ *Assuming that all the participating countries follow the international agreement on climate change to the letter, the hole in the Ozone layer will not disappear until some fifty years later.*

follow suit ① (of someone) to do the same thing as someone else does ▣ *If my sister decided to have noodles for lunch, I would follow suit.*

fool's gold ① It is a foolish plan for making money, which is doomed to failure. ▣ *It will more often be fool's gold to just buy shares in the stock market without doing research on the companies concerned.*

foot the bill ① (of someone) to pay for something ▣ *Just order whatever foods you like, and I shall foot the bill for the dinner tonight.*

for good measure ① as well ▣ *I understand that it is your good intention to visit us during the Chinese New Year. I suggest that you pay a visit to grandmother who lives nearby, for good measure.*

force someone's hand ① (of someone else) to make someone do something unwillingly or before the time that they are ready to do ▣ *I am reluctant to buy a new computer, but a real bargain that is very attractive has forced my hand.*

from head to foot ① covering the whole of someone's body ▣ *She dressed her son John in green from head to foot.*

from head to toe ① covering the whole of someone's body ▣ *We should all dress ourselves in black from head to toe when attending the funeral.*

from hell ① used after a noun to say that something or someone is extremely bad or unpleasant ▣ *He is a cook from hell. He adds too much salt and sugar into the dishes he makes.*

from nowhere ① very unexpectedly or suddenly ▣ *The truck came from nowhere and hit me although I looked both ways before crossing and saw nothing.*

from rags to riches ① It is used to depict the life of someone who was very poor in his youth and who later became very successful and rich. ▣ *This is a television documentary on the man who has gone from rags to riches.*

from the word go ① (of an activity) from the time when it is started ▣ *My marriage to Richard was a terrible mistake from the word go.*

from thin air ① (of something happened) quickly and unexpectedly ▣ *The stock market crash of October 1987 happened from thin air.*

from top to bottom ① thoroughly ▣ *She vacuumed up the dust and dirt in the carpets of all the rooms in the house from top to bottom.*

from top to toe ① It is used for describing someone whose entire body is covered in a particular thing or clothed in a particular clothing. ▣ *My father was dressed in brown from top to toe.*

G

gain ground ① (of something) to become more accepted, popular, or successful ▣ *The proposed idea of allowing the economic migrants into Australia lobbied by some community leaders is steadily gaining ground.*

gather dust ① (of something) to have not been used or to not be dealt with for a very long time ▣ *This office is empty and has been gathering dust for the last five years.*

get a bad press ① (of someone) to be criticised many times, especially on television, on radio, or in the newspapers ▣ *The president of the United States got a bad press for vetoing the bill about the economic relief package already passed by Congress.*

get a fix on someone ① (of someone else) to have a clear understanding of what someone is really like ▣ *I get a fix on one of my friends called John because I have known him for a long time.*

get a fix on something ① (of someone) to have a clear understanding or idea of what something is really like ▣ *I find it difficult to get a fix on the current situation.*

get a foot in the door ① (of someone) to make a small but successful start at something such as starting a new business which gives them a chance of doing well in the future ▣ *I landed a job in marketing earlier this year, and this would help me get a foot in the door when I will start my own business in the future.*

get a jump on someone ① (of someone else) to do something earlier than usual or well before someone does so as to get an edge over them ▣ *Our store manager gets a jump on its rivals as it holds winter sales promotion much earlier than them.*

get a raw deal ① (of someone) to be treated badly or unjustly ▣ *The Banking Commissioner said that banking customers got a raw deal from the major banks, and that the government would consider to pass new legislation to protect these customers.*

get away with murder ① (of someone) to be able to do whatever they want, even the things that are illegal or sinful, without being punished, criticised, or controlled ▣ *Do not let your kids get away with murder otherwise you will spoil them. You should punish or scold them when they are naughty or make mistakes.*

get brownie points ① (of someone) to earn appreciation or approval for something favourable or good that they have done for someone else ▣ *Peter was able to get brownie points with his girlfriend by cooking her a surprise lunch for her birthday.*

get egg on someone's face ① (of someone) to feel ashamed of themself or feel embarrassed because they have done or said something that they should not have in the first place ▣ *The government got egg on its face as it would cancel its plan to reduce subsidies for the rice industry that met with strong protest from the general public.*

get even with someone ① (of someone else) to exact their revenge on someone ▣ *Given that Peter has been maltreated by his boss since he worked for the company, he decides to tender his resignation tomorrow just to get even with him.*

get in on the act ① (of someone) to take or win advantage of something that was started by someone else ▣ *The staff in the IT department did all the hard work of automating the word tables for data insertion and extraction, and the staff in other departments now want to get in on the act.* ② (of someone) to take part in something that was started by someone else ▣ *Many new firms want to get in on the act and provide the best 5G phone plans for their potential customers.*

get into gear with something ① (of someone) to begin to deal with something effectively ▣ *The nation has got into gear with a campaign to reverse the climate change.*

get into your stride ① (of you) to become confident about or familiar with something you have started doing recently ▣ *You are getting into your stride and are doing all it can to fulfil your responsibilities.*

get off the hook ① (of someone) to succeed in getting out of the awkward situation that they were in without any blame or punishment ▣ *We shall not let Labor Party get off the hook for what it has done, and therefore we should vote for Coalition Party in the next election.*

get on like a house on fire ① (of two people) to like each other very much and have a very friendly relationship in a very short time ▣ *John introduced me to his father Ted, and we got on like a house on fire.*

get on someone's nerves ① (of someone else) to irritate or annoy someone, especially by doing something repetitively ▣ *Do not get on my nerves with these silly questions.*

get short shrift ① (of someone) to get no attention or sympathy or to get very little attention or sympathy ▣ *Customers who lodge too much complaints against the staff will often get short shrift.*

get something off your chest ① (of you) to talk to another person about something that has been a worrying issue or problem for you for a long time and you will feel better after talking about it ▣ *I note that you have a bad headache now. You had better see a doctor as soon as possible so that you will get it off your chest and have your headache treated.*

get something out of your system ① (of you) to allow yourself to express often a negative emotion or wish so that you can get rid of it and start to feel less angry or worried about it ▣ *If something bad* *happens to you, do let me know and I am certain that you would get it out of your system.*

get the boot ① (of someone) to be dismissed or fired from their job or position ▣ *Johnny got the boot when his boss had discovered that a computer had been stolen by him from the company.*

get the hang of something ① (of someone) to learn how to use or do something ▣ *I have never used a shredder before, but I think that I will get the hang of it after reading the instruction manual.*

get the picture ① (of someone else) to comprehend what someone is endeavouring to describe or explain to them ▣ *I told him about what had happened last night. He should get the picture.*

get the wooden spoon ① (of someone) to finish last in a competition or a race or to be the worst performer in a particular activity ▣ *Jenny ran the marathon in just under four hours but she got the wooden spoon.*

get to grips with something ① (of someone) to make an effort to understand something such as a problem or situation, and to deal with it directly and effectively ▣ *I will try to get to grips with using the latest technologies for my business.*

get to the bottom of something ① (of someone) to ascertain the underlying cause of something such as a mystery, a problem, or a situation before they can even attempt to deal with it ▣ *He will definitely try his best to get to the bottom of the cruise ship accident.* ② (of someone) to discover the truth about something such as a mystery, a problem, or a situation before they can even attempt to deal with it ▣ *She is determined to get to the bottom of the embezzlement of the company funds.*

get up someone's nose ① (of someone else) to annoy someone a lot ▣ *She got up my nose with her stupid questions.*

get wind of something ① (of someone) to hear or get to know about something secret or private, especially when other people did not want them to ▣ *I got wind of my uncle's divorce with his wife and his remarriage.*

get your act together ① (of you) to take action to become organised or prepared so that things could be done in a more efficient way ▣ *You will need to get your act together if you hope to win today.*

get your hands dirty ① (of you) to do physical work ▣ *It's not that the jobs aren't available, it's just that you don't want to get your hands dirty.*

get your hands on something ① (of you) to succeed in getting or finding something you want or need ▣ *I wondered why you were able to get your hands on that money so easily.*

get your head down ① (of you) to continue concentrating on and working hard at something ▣ *It is better for you to get your head down and try to finish your presentation report today so that you are ready to give your presentation tomorrow at the meeting.* ② (of you) to sleep ▣ *As a friend of yours, I will advise you to get your head down for at least seven hours every night.*

get your just deserts ① (of you) to deserve something unpleasant that already has happened to you, because you did something evil or immoral before ▣ *You should get your just deserts for committing a crime.*

get your marching orders ① (of you) to be ordered to leave a job or a place because you have done the wrong thing ▣ *I am sorry to hear that you have got your marching orders.*

get your own back on someone ① (of you) to take revenge on someone because of something that they have done to you in the past ▣ *I understand that Tony always bullied you at school, but you finally got your own back on him when you bought out his uncle's company and became his boss.*

get your teeth into something ① (of you) to become greatly involved with something and do it in an energetic and enthusiastic way ▣ *You were pleased that your boss delegated a project to you and you got your teeth into it with a view to completing it before the deadline.*

give as good as you get ① (of you) to argue, compete, criticise, or fight as confidently and fiercely as your opponent ▣ *You can give as good as you get in staff meetings.*

give lip service to something ① (of someone) to appear to support or agree with something without doing anything to prove or support it ▣ *The local council members gave lip service to the provision of assistance to the homeless people, but nobody did a follow up to see that they did what they had said.*

give me a break ① You only say this to show that you think someone is currently very annoying or ridiculous, or that you think their actions or behaviour are either annoying or ridiculous. ▣ *Albert, stop being a night owl all the time. Give me a break, will you? For the sake of your health, you should at least try to sleep before 11 p.m. and you should only wake up after 6 a.m.* ② You only say this to someone when they are annoying or criticising you, and you wish them to stop doing so and leave you alone. ▣ *Albert, I told you that I needed you to stop fiddling with your coins and keys while I was on a phone call with my manager, and you couldn't even do it for a few seconds! Give me a break, will you?*

give or take something ① (of the amount or the time mentioned) approximately ▣ *Lunch will be ready at noon, give or take 10 minutes.*

give someone a bell ① (of someone else) to give a telephone call to someone ▣ *Please do remind me to give my parents a bell this afternoon.*

give someone a blank cheque ① (of someone else) to give complete authority to someone to do what they think is best for themself ▣ *My boss has given me a blank cheque to do simple daily tasks.*

give someone a leg up ① (of someone else) to give someone an edge over other people so as to help them achieve something and become successful ▣ *Our school has a free after-school program that is intended to give students a leg up in any subjects they are having difficulty with.*

give someone a run for their money ① (of someone else) to not let someone win easily in a competition or contest ▣ *You should not underestimate your opponent today. They will give you a run for their money.*

give someone food for thought ① (of an idea) to make someone think long and hard about it ▣ *The idea raised at the meeting with the Chief Executive Officer of the company will give me food for thought. I might invest some money in the company via the stock market.*

give someone free rein ① (of someone else) to give someone the freedom to do what they need or want ▣ *The management gave John free rein to manage a newly formed department.*

give someone the benefit of the doubt ① (of someone else) to trust what someone is saying even though that they have strong reasons not to ▣ *He is the kind of person who always trusts other people. He makes it a practice to give everyone the benefit of the doubt.*

give someone the cold shoulder ① (of someone else) to ignore someone intentionally ▣ *His girlfriend gave his boyfriend the cold shoulder this week just to see what his reaction was.*

give someone the nod ① (of someone else) to give someone permission to do something ▣ *I gave Amanda the nod as I considered her to be the most qualified staff to undertake the project.*

give someone their head ① (of someone else) to allow someone to act in the way they want without giving them advice or stopping them ▣ *I gave my assistant his head to undertake the project that I had assigned to him.*

give something the thumbs down ① (of someone) to show their disapproval of an activity, a plan, a suggestion, and their unwillingness to accept it ▣ *I knew that my manager had approved my ideas but the Chief Executive Officer ultimately gave them the thumbs down.*

give something the thumbs up ① (of someone) to show their approval of an activity, a plan, a suggestion, and their willingness to accept it ▣ *Although the manager disapproved my ideas, the Chief Executive Officer ultimately gave it the thumbs up.*

give something your best shot ① (of you) to try your best to achieve something even though it may not be easy to do so ▣ *Though you had given it your best shot, you still got defeated in the tennis match.*

give the game away ① (of someone) to reveal something by saying or doing it in a way that lets someone else guess what the secret is ▣ *The actor did not intend to disclose his recent marriage to a wealthy woman but somehow the tabloid knew about this and gave the game away.*

give the thumbs down to something ① (of someone) to show their disapproval of an activity, a plan, a suggestion, and their unwillingness to accept it ▣ *The critics gave the thumbs down to his performance.*

give the thumbs up to something ① (of someone) to show their approval of an activity, a plan, a suggestion, and their willingness to accept it ▣ *The management finally gave the thumbs up to the project.*

gnash your teeth ① (of you) to complain about something in an angry, a noisy, and a very obvious way ▣ *When you had heard the news from you brother, you gnashed your teeth.*

go against the grain ① (of someone) to act contrary to their principles, beliefs or ideas, or to act in a manner that is not considered as normal or natural by others ▣ *I am an honest person and it goes against the grain not to tell the truth of the matter.*

go back to the drawing board ① (of someone) to begin doing something again from the beginning using a new approach after a previous failed attempt ▣ *My original plan does not work at all so I go back to the drawing board and consider other plans.*

go belly up ① (of a business or company) to stop operating because it does not have sufficient money to pay its debts ▣ *Because of not many sales and no working capital, the newly formed company goes belly up after just four months.*

go by the board ① (of a plan, an activity, or an idea) to be forgotten or stopped ▣ *Our plans to go to Europe last month for a holiday went by the board for lack of annual leave.*

go by the book ① (of someone) to do something exactly in accordance with the regulations or rules ▣ *The lawyers have to go by the book.*

go down the drain ① (of something) to be lost or spoiled, to become useless or wasted, or to fail ▣ *I needed to decide whether to rent or purchase a house. As regards renting, I felt that the money was virtually going down the drain every month, so I purchased a house instead.*

go down the pan ① (of something) to be lost or spoiled, to become useless or wasted, or to fail ▣ *You have destroyed my business because of your reckless spending. As a result, all those years of work have now gone down the pan.*

go down the tubes ① (of something) to be lost or spoiled, to become useless or wasted, or to fail ▣ *You need to have realistic plans for the project that you are undertaking otherwise monies spent on it will go down the tubes.*

go for a song ① (of something) to be sold very cheaply ▣ *I wanted to buy this book for a long time. When I noticed that it went for a song, I could not resist the temptation to buy it.*

go for broke ① (of someone) to risk everything by putting all their resources into and directing their efforts towards one idea or plan in the hope of having great success ▣ *The badminton team go for broke when there are only ten minutes left for the match.*

go for the jugular ① (of someone) to make every effort to defeat or attack someone else, usually by criticising or harming them very fiercely *As she does not like her main rival in tomorrow's tennis matches, she goes for the jugular well in advance of the game.*

go hand in hand ① (of two things) to be closely related in that they cannot be considered separately *At the community centre, I enrol my child in a playgroup where play and learning goes hand in hand.*

go head-to-head ① (of an organisation or a person) to be in direct competition with another organisation or person *Josephine will go head-to-head with her rivals in the tennis matches tomorrow.*

go into freefall ① (of a level or value of something) to begin to fall very fast and uncontrollably *The investment expert forecasts that shares could go into freefall before the end of the year.*

go into overdrive ① (of a group of people such as the media, or the cast) to start working very hard or performing well *When the human bones were discovered in my neighbour's backyard, the media went into overdrive by writing articles about the shocking discovery.*

go like clockwork ① (of something) to happen exactly as planned without any difficulties, problems, or trouble *The Christmas party went like clockwork last night.*

go off the rails ① (of a company or something) to begin to go wrong *By Summer, the plan for constructing a villa seemed to be going off the rails.* ② (of someone) to start behaving in a socially unacceptable or strange way *Jane went off the rails in Year 12 because she started to play truant.*

go on the record as saying ① (of someone) to say something officially or publicly so that it may be written down and reported *The actor has gone on the record as saying he will star in the new film 'Gorilla'.*

go out the window ① (of someone's particular way of behaving or thinking, a plan, a quality, or an idea) to disappear entirely *After two failures in the referendum on whether Australia is to become republic, the interest shown by the public in the subject goes out the window.*

go over someone's head ① (of someone else) to appeal to a person of higher position, level, or rank than someone in an attempt to get what they want *John's accounting manager Susan refuses to give John a day off so he goes over her head and speaks directly to the Alan* *who is the person in charge of the entire accounting department.* ② (of something) to be too difficult for someone to understand ▣ *The Quantum Field Theory will go over his head for his age.*

go pear-shaped ① (of a situation) to begin to deteriorate and bad things will start to appear ▣ *We played well in the first half of the game, but for some reason it went pear-shaped in the second half of the game and we ended up losing the match.* ② (of a situation or an activity) to go wrong ▣ *The whole thing went pear-shaped when the new project manager Peter had taken charge of the current project in our department.* ③ (of a plan) to fail ▣ *We had planned to go hiking in the lake district last weekend, but it went pear-shaped due to the torrential rain.*

go pop ① (of someone or something) to explode with a sudden short sound ▣ *The balloons that suddenly went pop awakened me.*

go the distance ① (of someone) to complete what they have commenced ▣ *The tennis player failed to go the distance as he withdrew from the match in the final round because of leg injury.*

go the whole hog ① (of someone) to do something as completely as possible ▣ *Let us go the whole hog and buy a carton of beers from the supermarket to celebrate my son who has been admitted into a famous University.*

go through hell ① (of someone) to have a very difficult or unpleasant time ▣ *When she was in secondary school, she went through hell. All other students in her class teased her because she was too fat.*

go through the motions ① (of someone) to do something because they are expected to do or have to do without making any, real effort, or being enthusiastic about it ▣ *Many of the office workers who did their jobs five days in a week were just going through the motions.*

go through the roof ① (of a level of something) to increase abruptly and very rapidly to a very high level ▣ *Buyers are selling their gold coins for cash because the gold prices here have gone through the roof.* ② (of someone) to suddenly become very annoyed or angry and usually vent their anger by shouting at someone else ▣ *Alex, just put the porcelain vase back before mum sees it and goes through the roof!*

go to pieces ① (of someone's work or relationship) to be no longer as good as it once was and they cannot prevent it from becoming worse ▣ *Their relationship began to go to pieces because they always* *argue over petty things.* ② (of someone) to be so afraid, nervous, sad, or upset that they cannot behave, live, think, or work normally ▣ *Mary just went to pieces after the death of her husband Barry.* ③ (of someone) to be so upset or sad by something that they cannot think clearly and control their emotions ▣ *Helen went to pieces when she was told by the doctor that she had breast cancer.*

go to the country ① (of someone) to demand that a general election to be held ▣ *The Prime Minister went to the country just to please the voters who were dissatisfied with his overall policies.*

go to the wall ① (of a company) to be destroyed financially ▣ *Because of the national lockdown, a total of about 2,000 companies went to the wall in the six months to December.*

go to way of all flesh ① (of someone) to die ▣ *The criminal went to way of all flesh after a police officer had shot him in the head for resisting arrest.*

go to your head ① (of alcohol) to quickly make you feel drunk in such a way that may influence your judgement with the result that you begin to act in a stupid way ▣ *The alcoholic drinks will definitely go to your head if you don't stop binge drinking right now.* ② (of you) to think that you are better or more important than others due to your own success, and later begin to act foolishly or arrogantly ▣ *If you are too complacent with your own success, you might run the risk of going to your head in the future.*

go under the hammer ① (of something) to be offered for sale at an auction ▣ *Richardson has got a lot of antiques at home that will go under the hammer next week.*

go up in smoke ① (usually of a building) to be destroyed completely by fire ▣ *This high-rise apartment building went up in smoke yesterday due to an arson attack.* ② If your plans go up in smoke, it means that you are not successful in achieving your plans. ▣ *The plan to expand my large business overseas at this time has gone up in smoke due to the strict investment and taxation laws that are imposed by the foreign governments.*

go with the flow ① to do what other people want you to do without exercising control over what happens to yourself ▣ *Just relax and go with the flow.*

grasp the nettle ① (of someone) to tackle a problem or unpleasant task in a determined way and without delay ▣ *Carmen needs to grasp the nettle of her company's computer system upgrade.*

greet someone with open arms ① (of someone else) to show someone that they are very happy to see them ▣ *I greeted my old friend with open arms.*

grin from ear to ear ① (of someone) to grin a lot and show their great happiness ▣ *They will soon get married. No wonder they grin from ear to ear.*

grist to the mill ① It is something that can be used to someone's advantage, or can be of use to someone for a particular purpose. ▣ *I might as well learn how to read stock charts because it is all grist to the mill when I choose what to invest in the stock market.*

grit your teeth ① (of you) to be determined to continue doing something in a situation that is either difficult or unpleasant ▣ *I note that you meet several problems in undertaking the project and there are unfortunately no simple solutions. I am afraid that you need to work hard to solve them. You would just have to grit your teeth and get on with it.*

H

hand in hand ① (of two people) holding each other's hand ▣ *My parents walked through the botanic garden hand in hand the other day.*

hang tough ① (of someone) to continue fighting or competing fiercely for something with the refusal to accept defeat ▣ *Donald Trump is hanging tough in order to get re-elected as the President of United States for another four years.*

hard on someone's heels ① (of someone else) to follow close behind someone, often to catch or chase them ▣ *With the enemy hard on their heels, the army crossed the river and they were now out of danger as the army were out of the enemy's cannon firing range.*

have a ball ① (of someone) to enjoy themself very much ▣ *Let us go to my girlfriend's dance party and have a ball there.*

have a card up your sleeve ① (of you) to have something such as a plan or an idea that is advantageous to you and can be used when the need arises in a particular situation, but it is not known by other people ▣ *You have a card up your sleeve when it is necessary to launch new products next month.*

have a chip on your shoulder ① (of you) to become easily angry or offended about something because you consider yourself to be treated unfairly in the past ▣ *I can see that you have a chip on your shoulder because you have not received an invitation to your best friend's dance party.*

have a crack at something ① (of someone) to make an attempt at achieving, doing, or winning something that usually involves a low to a high level of difficulty ▣ *I have decided to have a crack at the Sydney Marathon.*

have a field day ① (of someone) to take advantage of an opportunity or a situation to do something enjoyable ▣ *When there is an economic recession, a lot of the working class loses their jobs and thus are heavily in debt. Debt collectors are having a field day in the recession.*

have a free hand ① (of someone) to freely decide on how something should be done ▣ *Being the manager in charge of the computer department in our company, I have a free hand and am able to provide training to my subordinates in the way I like.*

have a go at someone ① (of someone else) to criticise someone, often in a severe way and without justification ▣ *Please stop having a go at me, otherwise I will be furious.*

have a hand in something ① (of someone) to be one of the people who are involved in creating or doing something ▣ *John has a hand in setting up a heating system.*

have a lot on your plate ① (of you) to have a lot of work to do ▣ *I am surprised that you have a lot on your plate every day since working in our IT department.* ② (of you) to have a whole host of problems to worry about or deal with ▣ *If you don't deal with your current problems properly right now, you are likely to have a lot on your plate later.*

have a lump in your throat ① (of you) to have a tight feeling in your throat that is due to anger, anxiety, sadness, sorrow, or another strong emotion ▣ *If you do know who is spreading rumours about you in the workplace, you will definitely have a lump in your throat.*

have a nose for something ① (of someone) to have a natural ability to find something ▣ *I have a nose for bargains whenever I go shopping.*

have a rough ride ① (of someone, or a group of people) to go through a rough time or a difficult situation ▣ *Businesses and communities are going to have a rough ride during the COVID-19 lockdown.*

have a running battle with someone ① (of someone else) to have an argument or a fight that lasts over several different occasions with someone ▣ *I have had a running battle with the neighbours over whose responsibility it is to pay for the fence.*

have a skeleton in the closet ① (of someone) to have an embarrassing or a scandalous secret ▣ *It is not surprising that most families have a skeleton in the closet but my mother does not disclose this to me.*

have a skeleton in the cupboard ① (of someone) to have an embarrassing or a scandalous secret ▣ *My mother told me that our family had a skeleton in the cupboard but she did not disclose this to me.*

have a soft spot for someone ① (of someone else) to care about or show a liking for someone a lot ▣ *My grandmother has a soft spot for one of her grandchildren, Josephine.*

have a sweet tooth ① (of someone) to like eating foods that have the taste of sweetness or that are high in sugar ▣ *Margaret has a sweet tooth and cannot resist eating chocolate bars.*

have an axe to grind ① (of someone) to argue for a particular cause due to their own private or selfish reasons ▣ *Politicians are often blamed or criticised by others for having an axe to grind.* ② (of someone) to be involved in something or do something due to their own private or selfish reasons ▣ *Albert is an environmentalist who doesn't have an axe to grind because he purely wants to teach other people how to look after the environment properly by giving them the right advice on recycling, saving water and electricity, using reusable products, using less paper, reducing food wastage, and so on.* ③ (of someone) to exhibit particular attitudes and prejudices about something, often for selfish reasons ▣ *There's no point in asking someone who has an axe to grind for any objective advice that you might need from them.*

have an eye for something ① (of someone) to be good at judging or noticing something, especially the one that they think it is attractive, of good quality, or valuable to them ▣ *I noticed that John had an eye for a bargain.*

have enough on your plate ① (of you) to have a lot of work to do *You already have enough on your plate and no one should be giving you more work to do.* ② (of you) to have a whole host of problems to worry about or deal with *You are not likely to have enough on your plate if you are willing to solve your own problems in a timely and proper manner.*

have green fingers ① (of someone) to be very good at gardening and can make plants grow well *My husband has green fingers and he spends a few hours in the garden every day.*

have had your fill of something ① (of you) to have experienced or done something that is especially unpleasant so that you do not want it any more *You must have had your fill of noises of the passing trains while staying in the resort hotel.*

have money ① (of someone) to be rich *Her cousin is known to have money.*

have never looked back ① It is used for describing someone who has never regretted about a decision that they make about something. *Josephine and Irene are now famous actresses and have never looked back.*

have no truck with something ① (of someone) to show their strong disapproval of something and their refusal to become involved with it *My boss assigned to me a project but I had no truck with it. This was because the plan was impractical and also the timetable for completion was unrealistic.*

have something at your fingertips ① (of you) to have something such as the facts or information that you can easily find, get, or refer to, and quickly use in a particular situation *With the use of the CommSec website, you will have all the up-to-date stock market news at your fingertips.*

have something in your sights ① (of you) to be aiming or striving to achieve something, and to have a high likelihood of success *For today's table tennis match, you have the victory in your sights.*

have something under your belt ① (of you) to have already achieved or done something important or useful *After a few years of intense study on grammatical rules, you have had enough materials under your belt to put them into a book.*

have something up your sleeve ① (of you) to have secret ideas or plans that will be used when the need arises or when the timing is right

have the last laugh ① (of someone) to finally win an argument after their critics or opponents have criticised them or have said that they would fail ▣ *Men have argued that they are safer drivers than women, but the recent car accident statistics have revealed that women drivers are less likely than men drivers to have a car accident. As a result, women drivers out there should have the last laugh on men drivers.* ② (of someone) to succeed in something after their critics or opponents have criticised them or have said that they would fail ▣ *The success of her new film that was directed by Tina meant that she had the last laugh on the movie critics who had said nasty things about her new film before.*

have the measure of someone ① (of someone else) to become aware of someone's strengths and weaknesses in order to make it easy for them to deal with or defeat someone ▣ *The golf player has the measure of his strong rivals and has several tricks up his sleeve in order to win them in the next matches.*

have time on your hands ① (of you) to have nothing to do or to have free time to do something else for a particular period ▣ *Although you often have time on your hands, you should not use your computer, mobile phone, and tablet for more than a few hours daily because the blue light emitted from these devices could damage your eyes in the long run.*

have tunnel vision ① (of someone) to direct their energy and skills towards focusing on the task that they think is the most important to them and ignore the things that other people might consider as important ▣ *If you would like to become an Australian golf champion, you must have tunnel vision.*

have your back to the wall ① (of you) to be in a difficult situation in which your ability to act is limited ▣ *Owing to the limited budget, you as the manager have your back to the wall and have no choice but to shelve the proposed plan.*

have your cake and eat it ① (of you) to do two things that are impossible to do at the same time ▣ *You can't have your cake and eat it - if you welcome your new customers to your store for the first time, you can't just stand there without asking them whether or not they will need your assistance or guidance.* ② (of you) to have two things that are impossible to have at the same time ▣ *You can't have your cake* *and eat it - if you have no time to work full-time five days a week, you won't have enough money to save for the future.*

have your finger on the pulse of something ① (of you) to always know the most up-to-date changes or developments in a particular situation or an activity to fully understand how something works ▣ *I understand that you emigrated to Australia from Hong Kong about 20 years ago. After such a long time here, I think that you have your finger on the pulse of Australia.*

have your hands full ① (of you) to be very or completely busy ▣ *You have your hands full so I ask your two younger brothers not to disturb you.*

have your work cut out ① (of you) to be likely to have difficulty in doing something ▣ *You will have your work cut out to wake up by four o'clock so as to catch the first train to the city.*

heads will roll ① It is used to mean that the people who are responsible or the people in authority are punished for something that has gone astray. ▣ *When the head teacher sees the damaged classroom because of naughty students, heads will roll.*

hear something on the grapevine ① (of someone) to hear about something because the information has been passed from one person to another during the conversation ▣ *The manager heard something on the grapevine that the government was about to sue our company over violation of the employment laws.*

hear something through the grapevine ① (of someone) to hear about something because the information has been passed from one person to another during the conversation ▣ *I heard something through the grapevine that my boss had resigned over his failure to complete an important project on time and within budget. Is this true or not?*

heave a sigh of relief ① (of someone) to feel happy because something that is worrying or unpleasant has not happened or has ended ▣ *The construction workers heave a sigh of relief when the building is completed on time.*

hedge your bets ① (of you) to lower your chances of suffering a loss or ending in failure by trying several different possibilities instead of one ▣ *You as a political commentator are hedging your bets about the likely outcome of this Saturday's election.*

hit home ① (of a situation or what someone says) to be accepted or realised by people, often painfully, that it is real or true ▣ *The horror of the war hit home when we saw the pictures on television at home.*

hit it off ① (of two people) to like each other as soon as they meet because they have many things in common, such as the same interests, same attitudes, and so on ▣ *John and Mary hit it off as soon as they met for the first time in their friend's birthday party.*

hit rock bottom ① (of something such as prices or sales) to be at the lowest bottom possible and be unlikely to go any lower ▣ *The prices of these old oil paintings hit rock bottom.* ② (of someone) to be in an unsuccessful, a hopeless, or a difficult situation that makes them feel very unhappy ▣ *When Peter was kicked out of the house by his girlfriend, he hit rock bottom.*

hit the big time ① (of someone) to become famous or successful or both ▣ *The fashion designer hit the big time in 1940 when she was chosen to design the wedding dress for the Queen.*

hit the bottle ① (of someone) to start drinking heavily and regularly ▣ *She was deeply depressed after knowing that her husband had been diagnosed with lung cancer, and this horrible news had caused her to hit the bottle.*

hit the ceiling ① (of someone) to become very angry ▣ *Susan will hit the ceiling if you continue to use abusive language to her.*

hit the jackpot ① (of someone) to make or win plenty of money all of a sudden ▣ *He seems to have hit the jackpot with the lottery that he bought yesterday at the newsagent.*

hit the road ① (of someone) to begin a journey ▣ *Maria has to hit the road at 5 a.m. in the morning because her company is in Central Business District and she starts work at 7 a.m.*

hit the roof ① (of someone) to become very angry ▣ *The parents will definitely hit the roof if they find out that their children have been playing truant from school.*

hold court ① (of someone) to receive a great deal of attention from other people who surround them because they are either their admirers or the people who think they are important or interesting ▣ *Josephine gets used to holding court in the company's canteen from a number of her colleagues as they always seek her help in solving their problems in the jobs.*

hold someone at bay ① (of someone else) to prevent someone unpleasant or an enemy from coming close to them or harming them ▣ *The police officer held the armed gunman at bay in an exchange of gunfire.*

hold someone to ransom ① (of someone else) to use their authority or influence to pressure someone into doing something they do not want to do ▣ *The doctors, who are currently working in public hospitals, hold the government to ransom by threatening to strike if it does not revoke its earlier decision of a pay cut.*

hold something at bay ① (of something done by someone) to prevent something dangerous, serious, or unpleasant from affecting them, from coming too close to them, from happening to them, or from harming them ▣ *Eating a balanced diet will hold diabetes at bay.*

hold the purse strings ① (of someone) to have control over how the money is used in a particular organisation, country, or family ▣ *Although my wife is not the breadwinner, she holds the purse strings in the family.*

hold your breath ① (of you) to be waiting anxiously or excitedly for something to happen ▣ *It seems that you hold your breath while your teacher is reading out the final examination results.*

hold your own ① (of you) to not become sicker or weaker in terms of your health ▣ *You have been ill for a week but you seem to hold your own.*

hot air ① false claims and promises ▣ *I do not believe a word that he says because he makes hot air all the time.*

hot on someone's heels ① (of someone else) to follow close behind someone, often to catch or chase them ▣ *After the bank robbery, the three criminals were running with five policemen hot on their heels.*

if it ain't broke, don't fix it ① It is used to mean that someone should not try to change, correct, fix, or improve something that is already working adequately well or that is in a satisfactory state. ▣ *The management is considering implementing these ridiculous changes. However, our current method is working just fine, and if it ain't broke, do not fix it. I suggest that my boss should relay this to the management immediately.*

if push comes to shove ① when a situation reaches a crucial point and someone must make a decision on how to continue ▣ *If push comes to shove, you sell the house. Although it is not ideal, it will give you enough money to pay the rent.*

I'll eat my hat ① (of you) to say with certainty that something will not happen at all ▣ *If he actually proposes to her, I'll eat my hat.*

in a good state of repair ① in good condition ▣ *My computer is in a good state of repair, and I don't need to purchase a new one for the time being.*

in a huff ① (of someone) angry and offended ▣ *I was in a huff because my boyfriend had forgotten my birthday and I could not believe it because it was simply ridiculous.*

in a position of authority ① (of someone) having the power to make important decisions officially ▣ *During the Annual General Meeting, everyone in a position of authority agreed to the sale of a factory.*

in a vacuum ① not affected by the influences from the outside or the external sources of information ▣ *The management implements these policies in a vacuum so it is no wonder that many employees are unhappy about them.*

in all weathers ① (of something done by someone) in every type of weather ▣ *She goes out for a walk after every meal in all weathers.*

in black and white ① in writing ▣ *I am pleased that I get your verbal offer but I also need to receive it in black and white.*

in cold blood ① (of someone who kills someone else) in a way that appears to show only cruelty and not show any emotions ▣ *One of the young shoplifters was shot dead by a police officer in cold blood inside a supermarket but the other one was caught on the spot.*

in fine fettle ① (of someone) healthy or strong ▣ *I am very delighted to be informed that both of my parents are in fine fettle.* ② (of something) in good condition ▣ *The sofa that we have been using since 2000 is still in fine fettle.*

in fits and starts ① not happening continuously, but alternating between starting and stopping ▣ *We made a series of presentations to help the public fully understand our new system but the disappointment was that we presented them in fits and starts.*

in front of your eyes ① If something happens in front of your eyes, it happens directly before you where you can see it clearly and you cannot do anything to change it or stop it. ▣ *The three armed robbers killed five customers in front of your eyes while committing the bank robbery.*

in good fettle ① (of someone) healthy or strong ▣ *I am very delighted to know that you are in good fettle today.* ② (of something) in good condition ▣ *I am surprised that your old printer is still in good fettle after you have been using for five years.*

in high places ① It is used to describe people as having influential and powerful positions in a society, an organisation, or the government. ▣ *You will not be promoted to a department manager so high, so fast without your uncle and aunt in high places.*

in inverted commas ① It is used to say literally that a particular phrase or word is neither an accurate nor a suitable description. ▣ *All her friends, in inverted commas, disappeared when she was declared bankrupt.*

in leaps and bounds ① (of something that develops, grows, improves, or progresses) very quickly ▣ *Australian population grew in leaps and bounds as it approved about 200,000 immigrants each year.*

in one's blood ① It is used to mean that it is natural for one to do something because it has been done in the past by one's family. ▣ *Alexander has tennis in his blood possibly because his father is a world tennis champion.*

in one's book ① according to one's own code of personal ethics, judgment, or opinion ▣ *My sister says that John is very stupid, but he is fairly clever in your book.*

in safe hands ① protected from danger or harm by a particular organisation or person ▣ *Our two kids are now in safe hands while we are at work because they are well looked after by our close relative.*

in someone's hands ① under the control of someone or in someone's possession ▣ *Some Ministers have criticised the recent change in policies, saying that this will leave too much power in Prime Minister's hands.*

in something's wake ① (of an event) that causes or leaves behind an unpleasant situation after that event has happened ▣ *An ambulance that sped past our car emitted a wisp of smoke in its wake.*

in spades ① in large amounts or to a great degree ▣ *Intelligence, looks, wealth, wisdom - her son had all of them in spades.*

in the air ① being expressed or felt by many people ▣ *A sense of excitement as a result of live entertainment was in the air in China Town during the Chinese New Year in Australia.* ② It is used for describing something that is about to happen. ▣ *Tax reform is in the air.*

in the balance ① It is used to mean that what is going to happen in a situation is not clear. ▣ *The fate of these two immigrants who committed the gang rape of a 15-year-old girl continues to be in the balance.*

in the doldrums ① In the case of an industry, a company, or an activity, it is not doing well, not developing, or not successful. ▣ *The tourist industry is in the doldrums after the national lockdown as a result of the outbreak of the coronavirus pandemic.*

in the front line of something ① with a significant role to play in the achievement or the defence of something ▣ *I am in the front line of the project that my supervisor delegated to me two months ago.*

in the heat of the moment ① (of someone) without thinking about what they are doing or saying because of anger or excitement ▣ *It was seldom that Mary used bad language to scold the journalist who reported false news about her. She was in the heat of the moment.*

in the hot seat ① (of someone) in a difficult position where they have to make important decisions, answer questions, etc. ▣ *He has spent five years in the hot seat as the Chief Executive Officer of a big supermarket named Woolworths.*

in the line of duty ① (of someone) while doing their job ▣ *Several firemen were injured in the line of duty yesterday evening.*

in the market for something ① (of someone) interested in buying or obtaining something ▣ *If you are in the market for expensive person care products, I shall provide you with a list of the most well-known brands for your free choice.*

in the middle of nowhere ① (of someone) a long way from any other place ▣ *When I was just five years old, my family moved away from the city to the suburb in the middle of nowhere.*

in the nick of time ① just before it is too late or just in time before something bad happens ▣ *John woke up in the nick of time to leave his home that was on fire.*

in the pipeline ① It is used for describing something such as a plan, an event, or an idea that is being discussed, planned, or prepared and that is bound to happen in the near future. ▣ *As a result of the restructuring of our company, more job losses were in the pipeline.*

in the same breath ① (of someone) to say that someone else has said two contradictory things at the same time ▣ *He strongly criticised the play. However, he predicted in the same breath that it would be a great success ultimately.*

in the thick of something ① (of someone) engaged in the most active or the busiest part of something ▣ *He suddenly found himself in the thick of an argument erupted in the dance party.*

in the throes of something ① (of someone or a company) doing or experiencing something that is difficult, painful, or unpleasant ▣ *The company's future looks bleak. It is in the throes of a six-month-old strike and is losing nearly two million dollars a day.*

in the wake of something ① It means that an earlier event, often an unpleasant one, has led to something to happen after it and is usually the cause of it. ▣ *The general strike in the company follows in the wake of its failure to improve the hygiene as promised by the management earlier this year.*

in the wilderness ① If someone is in the wilderness, it means that they no longer have the power at a particular time. ▣ *The former president was in the wilderness, which was reflected by his recent presidential election loss, because he had mishandled the COVID-19 pandemic.* ② If someone is in the wilderness, it means that they either no longer have a position of authority or no longer have an important position. ▣ *Jane was finally given a government position after five years in the wilderness.* ③ If someone is in the wilderness, it means that they no longer have an involvement in something important at a particular time. ▣ *Tom is in the wilderness because he has ended his political career due to his early retirement.*

in the works ① being in progress or being planned ▣ *The City Development Department says that a casino and a hotel are in the works.*

in triplicate ① (of documents) in three copies ▣ *Please do complete the forms in triplicate.*

in your element ① (of you) doing something that you find enjoyable or do best ◾ *You must be in your element, boiling the eggs for the dinner.*

in your heart of hearts ① If you believe, know, or feel something in your heart of hearts, it means that you believe, know, or feel it is true despite being reluctant to accept it. ◾ *You knew in your heart of hearts that your brother shoplifted in a supermarket yesterday.*

in your mind's eye ① in your memory or imagination, especially referring to something that is being visualised ◾ *In your mind's eye, you can imagine what it is like when going to jail.*

in your right mind ① (of you) being rational and behaving sensibly ◾ *In your right mind, you would not agree to sign this contract containing those kinds of terms.*

it's a good job that ① it is lucky that ◾ *It's a good job that you brought a bottle of sunblock with you this morning.*

it's a toss-up ① (of a situation in which either of two choices, either of two possibilities, or either of two results) to be equally likely or possible ◾ *I don't have a clue who'll be promoted to a warehouse manager, and it's a toss-up between James and Peter.*

it's early day ① It is too early to be sure of what will happen in the future. ◾ *The chances of Australia eventually becoming a republic are perhaps higher this time after two unsuccessful attempts. It's early day because the counting of the voting results hasn't finished yet.*

it's not the end of the world ① It is used to tell someone that a problem is not as bad or unpleasant as they thought ◾ *Do not worry about losing your job. It's not the end of the world.*

it's touch and go ① It is something that someone has no certainty of knowing whether it will happen or not. 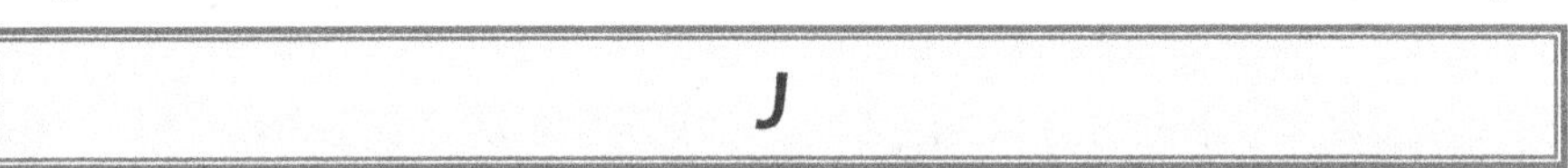 *I think our football team is going to beat the team B in the match tomorrow but it's touch and go.*

J

jump on the bandwagon ① (of someone) to start participating in an activity, which is becoming fashionable and in which others are finding success while or after doing it, in the hope of becoming either famous or successful, or reaping some benefits ◾ *Our company manufactured only 500 pieces of this product for trial sales over the* *internet. The fact that the goods were snapped up within one hour of the sales led to many other companies to jump on the bandwagon.*

jump ship   ① (of someone) to leave an organisation where they are working to join another one ▣ *As John is not happy with the working environment in his current workplace, he intends to jump ship.*

jump the gun   ① (of someone) to do something before the expected or proper time ▣ *We have just known each other, but Richard is already talking about marriage next month. Is he jumping the gun?*

just around the corner   ① going to happen soon ▣ *Life seems to be bit rough for me at the moment, but I think that the good times are just around the corner.* ② near or very near ▣ *There is a great shopping centre just around the corner.*

just for the hell of it   ① for no particular reason other than for pure enjoyment ▣ *My son-in-law plays golf just for the hell of it.*

just round the corner   ① going to happen soon ▣ *I have recently been informed that my promotion to the position of manager is just round the corner.* ② near or very near ▣ *There is a fantastic garden centre just round the corner.*

just the tip of the iceberg   ① It is the small and the noticeable part of a much larger problem or situation that may not yet be obvious. ▣ *The protests against the national lockdown because of the coronavirus pandemic are just the tip of the iceberg.*

just to be on the safe side   ① It is used for describing someone who does something beforehand in case something undesirable happens, although this may be unnecessary. ▣ *You probably don't need to apply for council permission to build a small pergola in your backyard, but you had better check with the council first just to be on the safe side.*

K

keep a cool head   ① (of someone) to remain calm in a frightening, or dangerous situation or when they are in a predicament ▣ *One should keep a cool head when trying to find a way out of an undesirable situation.*

keep a high profile   ① (of someone or a company) to get a lot of attention from the public ▣ *The star needs to keep a high profile in Australia.*

keep a low profile ① (of someone) to not do things that will attract other people's attention ■ *It is better for you to keep a low profile when doing something that might arouse your co-workers' jealousy.*

keep a stiff upper lip ① (of someone) to hide their emotions or feelings and not let other people know their own real emotions or feelings ■ *I am a person who will keep a stiff upper lip when I am feeling down and do not want to be disturbed by others.*

keep a straight face ① (of someone) to succeed in looking serious by refraining themself from laughing or smiling at something that is supposed to be funny ■ *I am surprised that he is able to keep a straight face when I have told him the funniest jokes.*

keep a tight rein on something ① (of someone) to exercise tight or strict control over something ■ *A clear indication of an economic downtown is that most consumers must have kept a tight rein on their spending.*

keep someone at arm's length ① (of someone else) to avoid becoming friendly or emotionally involved with someone ■ *He cannot trust Adam any more and is keeping him at arm's length.*

keep someone at bay ① (of someone else) to prevent someone unpleasant or an enemy from coming close to them or harming them ■ *John failed to keep his creditors at bay because he could not make the required monthly repayments on time.*

keep someone in the picture ① (of someone else or something used) to provide someone with all the information that they need to comprehend the situation or to ensure that someone knows all the facts that pertain to a changing situation ■ *I use the radio and television to keep me in the picture about what is happening in the world.*

keep someone on the straight and narrow ① (of someone else) to help someone to behave in a morally correct way ■ *It is important for the community to work together and keep the vulnerable young people on the straight and narrow.*

keep someone on their toes ① (of someone else or something) to cause or force someone to be ready and alert for any eventuality ■ *His manager has been keeping his staff on their toes by constantly teaching them new skills in handling all sorts of difficult scenarios.*

keep someone posted ① (of someone else) to regularly update someone with the information about something that concerns them ■ *It is the responsibility of an employees to keep their manager posted.*

keep someone sweet ① (of someone else) to try to keep someone satisfied and pleased with them so that they will treat them well in return ▣ *Some companies will keep their employees sweet so that they will work harder and happier.*

keep something at bay ① (of something done by someone) to prevent something dangerous, serious, or unpleasant from affecting them, from coming too close to them, from happening to them, or from harming them ▣ *Sleeping at least seven hours a day will keep most of the common illnesses at bay.*

keep something in mind ① (of someone) to remember something when they are doing something ▣ *Walking alone on city streets at night is dangerous, especially for woman, and we should keep this in mind.*

keep something under wraps ① (of someone) to keep something secret ▣ *The CIA has kept thousands of official reports on UFO findings under wraps for decades.*

keep tabs on someone ① (of someone else) to keep someone under close supervision ▣ *The police will keep tabs on certain suspects if they believe that they are the drug smugglers.*

keep the lid on something ① (of someone) to control a situation or to hide the problems so as to prevent it from becoming worse ▣ *The movie star was trying very hard to keep the lid on his extramarital affair with another movie star.*

keep track of something ① (of someone) to be certain that they have the latest and the most accurate information about something all the time ▣ *It is the responsibility of a business owner to keep track of the expenditures and revenues of their business.*

keep your cool ① (of you) to not lose your temper and remain calm in a difficult situation ▣ *You must learn to keep your cool no matter where you are.*

keep your eyes open ① (of you) to carefully watch so that you will become aware of when someone or something appears ▣ *While you are typing up this magazine article, keep your eyes open for any grammatical and spelling errors and correct them as you go.*

keep your feet on the ground ① (of you) to continue to do something practically and sensibly even when the exciting or new things are happening ▣ *You should remember to keep your feet on the ground by often staying in touch with your family and friends and not forgetting them just because exciting or new things are popping up in* *your film career time after time.* ② (of you) to continue to do something practically and sensibly even when you become powerful or successful ▣ *It is important for you to remember that you should always keep your feet on the ground no matter how much you have achieved in life so far.* ③ (of you) to have a realistic and sensible attitude to life ▣ *You should always keep your feet on the ground despite your overnight fame.*

keep your finger on the pulse of something ① (of you) to always know the most up-to-date changes or developments in a particular situation or an activity to fully understand how something works ▣ *You should keep your finger on the pulse of the coronavirus pandemic.*

keep your fingers crossed ① (of you) to hope that something will happen the way you expected or wanted ▣ *She will be having an operation on her knees today so keep your fingers crossed.*

keep your head ① (of you) to remain calm in a difficult, frightening, or dangerous situation ▣ *You should always keep your head under pressure.*

keep your head above water ① (of you) to manage to survive on your income or to keep your business ▣ *Because of the economic recession, you have been struggling for years to keep your head above water.*

keep your head down ① (of you) to behave quietly so that you do not want to be noticed by other people because you try to avoid involvement or trouble in a dangerous or difficult situation ▣ *Albert, you should keep your head down by not approaching this troublemaker.*

kick your heels ① (of you) to feel bored or impatient because you have to have nothing to do while you are waiting somewhere for someone or because someone is keeping you waiting on purpose ▣ *Someone has told me before that the film is scheduled to shoot in black and white this morning, but I have just found out that the main actor will only arrive in the afternoon so unfortunately you as a cameraman might kick your heels for several hours.*

kiss goodbye to something ① (of someone) to acknowledge the fact that they will lose something or that they will lose an opportunity to do something ▣ *After the truck accident, I am absolutely sure that I will have to kiss goodbye to my truck driving career.*

kiss-and-tell ① It is a public story in which someone divulges their love affair with a famous person. ▣ *John is going to publish a book about his kiss-and-tell stories.*

knock someone for six ① (of a company, someone else, or something) to give someone a shock or surprise from which they have difficulty in recovering ▣ *Losing his job because of downsizing by the company really knocks him for six.* ② (of something) to upset someone so much that they find it hard to deal with it ▣ *The news of my father's death knocked me for six.* ③ (of something such as an illness) to make someone feel very unwell ▣ *That fever really knocked me for six.*

knock someone into shape ① (of someone else) to take action to make someone better so that they are able to reach the required standard ▣ *Some of my subordinates lack experience and I have decided to provide more training to them in order to knock them into shape.*

knock something into shape ① (of someone else) to use whatever methods that are needed to change or ameliorate something in order to make it reach the required standard ▣ *The programmers were instructed to knock the existing accounting software into shape by rewriting or refactoring only part of the software to meet current accounting requirements stated by the accounting department.*

know something inside out ① (of someone) to be very familiar with something ▣ *Mary has played tennis for many years and she knows the game inside out.*

know the score ① (of someone) to understand the real facts of or the important facts in a situation, especially the unpleasant facts ▣ *You know the score - no bonus payments until after the probation period is over.*

L

land on your feet ① (of you) to get into a good situation not because you make an effort yourself but because you are lucky ▣ *I am not worried about you because you always land on your feet.*

larger than life ① (of someone) attracting a great deal of attention because they are more interesting or exciting than most people ▣ *Our children like uncle John very much as he is larger than life.*

late in the day ① possibly too late for taking appropriate action or behaving in a certain way to be considered as fully effective in doing something ▣ *It is probably a bit late in the day for anyone to raise objection to my suggestion.*

laugh at someone's expense ① (of someone else) to laugh at someone in a way that makes them look like a fool ▣ *I would never forget the people who laughed at my expense because I was fat and bald.*

laugh your head off ① (of you) to laugh loudly or very loudly for a long time ▣ *You will laugh your head off when you tune in to listen to some funny jokes.*

lay down the law ① (of someone) to tell other people what to do, how they should think, etc. in a very forceful, or impolite way ▣ *You can let your kid ride a bicycle only if you lay down the law and stick to it.*

lay something at someone's door ① (of someone else) to lay the blame on someone for something ▣ *I am not sure whether or not we can lay his death at doctor's door.*

lay something on the line ① (of someone) to do something which increases their risk of losing something such as their reputation or job ▣ *All my subordinates have been told to follow the set procedures in their daily work, but Mary lays her disobedience on the line.*

lay your hands on someone ① (of you) to catch someone who has committed a wrongful act ▣ *You are a brave policeman who has laid your hands on the armed shoplifter in this supermarket.*

lay your hands on something ① (of you) to succeed in getting or finding something that you want or need ▣ *Have you laid your hands on your car keys yet?*

lead the field ① It is used to describe that you are better than, more active than, or more successful than the other people who are involved in the same activity as you or who are in the same competition as you. ▣ *I hear that you lead the field in tennis coaching.*

learn the ropes ① (of someone) to learn all the things that they need to know in order to deal with a system, to do a particular job or task, or to do an activity ▣ *He will have to spend the first few weeks just to learn the ropes at his new job.*

leave a mark on someone ① to have a lasting effect on someone, which is usually a bad one ▣ *Such painful memories were bound to leave a mark on the prisoners of war victims.*

leave a mark on something ① to have a lasting effect on something, which is usually a bad one ▣ *The war that had caused the death of many civilians and soldiers left a mark on the country.*

leave its mark on someone ① to have a lasting effect on someone, which is usually a bad one ▣ *Such a frightening experience was bound to leave its mark on the plane crash survivors.*

leave its mark on something ① to have a lasting effect on something, which is usually a bad one ▣ *The outbreak of the bubonic plague that had nearly wiped out one-fifth of the London's population in the years between 1664 and 1665 left its marks on the country.*

leave no stone unturned ① (of someone) to consider or try every possible course of action with a view to achieving something ▣ *She left no stone unturned in her search for her biological mother.*

leave someone cold ① (of something) to fail to cause excitement or interest to someone ▣ *The comic opera leaves my partner cold.*

leave someone high and dry ① (of a situation) to leave someone in a predicament in which they cannot do anything about it ▣ *What left me high and dry was that I had missed the last bus home, and, as a result, I had to walk home in the rain.*

leave someone in the lurch ① (of someone else) to place someone in a predicament by abandoning or leaving them at a time when they do need them to stay and help them ▣ *Mary was indignant enough to quit his job without giving prior notice, leaving his boss in the lurch.*

leave someone out in the cold ① (of someone else) to ignore someone and not involve them in the activities that they are doing ▣ *My sister left me out in the cold when she went to the dancing party without me.*

leave someone to their own devices ① (of someone else) to allow someone to do what they want or make their own decisions about what to do ▣ *Although Alan is a new employee, I will leave him to his own devices because I think he is very clever.*

left something hanging in the air ① (of someone) to avoid the discussion of a question or a remark because they do not want to deal with it as well as any issues associated with it ▣ *The spokesperson left* *some important questions hanging in the air regarding the resignation of the marketing manager.*

lend a hand ① (of someone else) to help someone do something, especially something that requires some physical effort ▣ *If you lend a hand in the kitchen, I could prepare the dinner much faster.*

lend someone a hand ① (of someone else) to help someone do something, especially something that requires some physical effort ▣ *If you lend me a hand, I could get this done faster.*

let her rip ① (of someone) to make a boat, car, etc. go as fast as possible ▣ *Today is an ideal day for driving your new racing car on this empty racetrack, and it will be great if you can just put your foot on the accelerator and let her rip so that I could see how well it will perform.*

let off steam ① (of someone) to do or say something that helps them get rid of their anger, energy, or strong feelings ▣ *My wife walks briskly after work to let off steam.*

let something slip through your fingers ① (of you) to fail to take an offer or opportunity, especially something good ▣ *You should never let an opportunity slip through your fingers because it rarely comes twice.*

let your hair down ① (of you) to enjoy yourself in a relaxed manner without having to worry about behaving politely ▣ *I think that sometimes it is fine to let your hair down in a wild party.*

lick your wounds ① (of you) to feel pity or sympathy for yourself after suffering a complete defeat or humiliation ▣ *You must be licking your wounds after suffering a major defeat in the state election.* ② (of you) to spend time attempting to get back your confidence, happiness, or strength after a bad experience, a defeat, or a disappointment ▣ *You must be licking your wounds after failing a final examination.*

life in the fast lane ① It is a way of living that is full of activity and excitement, but that often involves a lot of dangers and pressure as well. ▣ *John has decided to move to the countryside and become a farmer instead, simply because he doesn't want to live the life in the fast lane any more.*

like clockwork ① at exactly the planned times ▣ *I promise my parents that I will call them every day like clockwork when I shall be in Wellington on business next week.* ② very regularly ▣ *The trains are running like clockwork due to the addition of the new trains to the existing railway network.*

line your pockets ① (of you) to get rich in an unfair or dishonest way ▣ *You will be sentenced up to 10 years imprisonment if you are caught to line your pockets.*

live a lie ① (of someone) to always pretend that they feel or believe something when it is not the case ▣ *People have to stop living a lie and be frank about how they feel.*

live from hand to mouth ① (of someone) to have barely enough to pay for the bare essentials or necessities and nothing extra ▣ *We live from hand to mouth because both of our parents are retired and rely heavily on the meagre age pension payments that are given weekly.*

live hand to mouth ① (of someone) to have barely enough to pay for the bare essentials or necessities and nothing extra ▣ *We live hand to mouth because both of our parents are very poorly paid by their employers.*

lock, stock, and barrel ① (of something) encompassing every part of something else ▣ *It would have been easier for him to sell his house lock, stock, and barrel.*

look at home ① It is used to mean that it is appropriate, natural, or usual for someone or something to be there. ▣ *The new round medium grey rug looks at home in our living room.*

look at something through rose-tinted spectacles ① (of someone) to notice only the good things about a situation and fail to notice the unpleasant things of it ▣ *You should always look at life through rose-tinted spectacles. As a result, you will live longer.*

look down your nose at someone ① (of you) to think that you are better than someone and treat them with contempt or disrespect ▣ *Do not look down your nose at these people just because they are homeless.*

look into the crystal ball ① (of someone) to say what will happen in the future about something ▣ *Without the experts to look into the crystal ball, it is difficult for other people to say whether or not the Australian economy will go out of recession next year.*

look on the bright side ① (of someone) to try to be cheerful about a bad situation by thinking that it is not as bad as it could have been or by thinking of the advantages that could possibly result from it ▣ *Albert failed to get a good mark in his examination but he looked on the bright side.*

look someone in the eye ① (of someone else) to look directly at someone's eyes in order to convince them that they are telling the truth or that they are not afraid of them ■ *After telling Mary about the whereabouts of her grandmother, I look her in the eye.*

look the other way ① (of someone) to intentionally ignore something illegal, immoral, or unpleasant that is happening ■ *John stole over $5,000 worth of computer equipment from his neighbour yesterday, but his friend looked the other way and did not tell the police about the theft.*

look the part ① (of someone) to look suitably for a particular job, occasion, position, role, or situation ■ *Alan looks the part for his new role as a treasurer in the company.* ② (of someone) to do well and seem likely to succeed ■ *Mary is starting to look the part on the tennis court.*

loose ends ① These are the parts of something that have not been completed, have not been done correctly, or have not been sorted out satisfactorily. ■ *Although Richard says that he has finished writing the memoir about Prince Charles, I think that there are still some loose ends to be tied up.*

lose ground ① (of someone) to become less popular than before, to be given lesser support than in the past, or to lose some of the advantages or power previously possessed by them ■ *The actor loses ground after he has been discovered to have an affair with another actress.*

lose heart ① (of someone) to begin to lose interest in something or to feel discouraged, usually because things do not progress in the way that they hoped for ■ *I lose heart in making aeroplanes models because I have neither the time nor the money to continue with this hobby.*

lose it ① (of someone) to become unable to control their emotions and suddenly start to cry, shout, or laugh ■ *A car slammed into my new mailbox, and I completely lost it after witnessing the whole accident myself.*

lose sight of something ① (of someone) to no longer pay attention to an important aspect, fact, or idea of something because they are preoccupied with something else of lesser importance ■ *It is very important that you do not lose sight of the real purpose of having a regular meeting.*

lose the plot ① (of someone) to behave in a silly or strange way and not know what to do ▣ *People should never lose the plot when they are working with dangerous and heavy machinery.* ② (of someone) to lose the ability to deal with or understand a situation, which is usually a difficult one ▣ *Peter seems to be losing the plot when I ask him about the reasons behind the ongoing saga of financial problems that our company is currently facing.*

lose track of something ① (of someone) to not know where something is, or what is happening to them any more ▣ *Any employee who has been assigned a task should never lose track of the task in terms of its progress.*

lose your cool ① (of you) to become angry, worried, or upset in an annoying situation, or in a difficult or frightening situation ▣ *Are you going to quit your job when you have finally lost your cool with your manager?*

lose your edge ① (of you) to lose your strong beliefs or opinions, energy, or skills that contributed to your prior success ▣ *Although you are a successful sole trader, you will lose your edge if you do not continue to sharpen your skills and do not keep yourself up-to-date in this competitive business environment.*

lose your grip ① (of you) to become less able or unable to deal with a situation due to no confidence or loss of confidence ▣ *Never look down on yourself if you don't want to lose your grip.*

lose your head ① (of you) to be in a state of panic and become unable to behave calmly or sensibly in a predicament ▣ *You should never lose your head whenever you are faced with danger.*

loud and clear ① (of something that is communicated with someone) in a way that is very easy to comprehend ▣ *We must ensure that our message came across loud and clear if we want our employees to do their work properly.*

lower your guard ① (of you) to stop being careful or staying alert, which you should not do to avoid danger or difficulty ▣ *You should never lower your guard when you are crossing the roads.*

M

make a clean sweep of something ① (of someone) to win a series of things or something with great ease ▣ *The world No. 1 tennis player* *made a clean sweep of the four grand slam tournaments this year.* ② (of someone) to initiate a complete change or make a lot of changes in a company or an organisation by removing all the ideas, methods, staff, or things that need changing or that are viewed as unnecessary ▣ *The new appointed Chief Executive Officer made a complete sweep of the conglomerate.*

make a dent in something ① (of something happened) to reduce an amount or the level of something, especially money or work ▣ *The economy is so bad during the COVID-19 pandemic in that many people have lost their jobs, which in turn will make a large dent in their income.*

make a face ① (of someone) to show their feeling such as disgust or dislike to someone else or something by making some strange facial expressions ▣ *I made a face at the man who was constantly licking his fingers while preparing the food.*

make a killing ① (of someone) to make a large profit very easily and quickly ▣ *My friend made a killing with the sale of his mansion.*

make a name for yourself ① (of you) to become well-known or famous as a result of doing a particular thing ▣ *I want to congratulate you on making a name for yourself as an outstanding author.*

make a pitch for something ① (of someone) to try to persuade people to support or buy something by telling them how good it is ▣ *The salesman used his persuasive words to make a pitch for the new products displayed in the store.* ② (of someone) to try to get something ▣ *To my surprise, Albert has decided to make a pitch for the job.*

make a splash ① (of someone) to suddenly become a very well-known or very successful ▣ *He made a splash at the press conference with his talks about his new novel.*

make both ends meet ① (of someone) to earn or have barely enough money to survive on, to buy the bare essentials or necessities, and to pay bills when due ▣ *When Josephine was unemployed, she could barely make both ends meet.*

make capital out of something ① (of someone) to use either a situation or an event for their own advantage ▣ *The Opposition has made capital out of the government's failure to finish building the new train stations on time and within budget.*

make ends meet ① (of someone) to earn or have barely enough money to survive on, to buy the bare essentials or necessities, and to pay bills when due ▣ *Most families living in developing countries are struggling every day to make ends meet.*

make headway ① (of someone) to make progress towards something that they are doing ▣ *I endeavour to learn how to play soccer but I am not making headway.*

make no bones about something ① (of someone) to do or talk about something very openly without feeling ashamed, embarrassed, nervous, or uncertain ▣ *My boss made no bones about his complete satisfaction with my performance in the job during the three-month probation period.*

make noises about something ① (of someone) to talk about something indirectly or vaguely ▣ *He made noises about the possibility of getting hired after the job interview.*

make someone's day ① (of good news or something good happened) to make someone feel very happy on the day ▣ *What really made John's day today is seeing his old best friends again.* ② (of good news or something good happened) to turn someone's day from a dull or ordinary one into a memorable and pleasing one for someone ▣ *I felt dull this morning, but what made my day was hearing the good news that my friend Adam from America would come and visit me this evening.*

make someone's hackles rise ① (of something) to cause anger, annoyance, or indignation to someone ▣ *His throwaway remarks were enough to make my hackles rise.*

make someone's toes curl ① (of someone else) to make someone feel very embarrassed or uncomfortable ▣ *My housemate makes my toes curl whenever he says inappropriate things.*

make the grade ① (of someone) to succeed in doing something usually by reaching the required standard ▣ *One of my students has failed to make the grade in the national literacy test.*

make waves ① (of someone) to deliberately cause trouble by changing or challenging the way something that is done ▣ *Do not make waves otherwise your employment will not last long.*

make your blood boil ① (of someone's action or something happened) to make you very angry ▣ *He made your blood boil when he blamed you for something you did not do.*

make your mark ① (of you) to do something that makes you famous or makes you become the centre of attention ▣ *To make your mark in this winter fashion show is such an easy task for you because you have so much experience in the fashion industry.*

make yourself at home ① (of you) to tell someone to feel comfortable and relax somewhere as if they were in a very familiar situation or you were in their own home ▣ *Just sit down in this sofa and make yourself at home.*

mark time ① (of troops) to march on the same spot without moving forward ▣ *The soldiers mark time in the ceremony today.* ② (of someone) to not do anything decisive or new while they are waiting for something that is going to happen ▣ *I am going to mark time while I am still working in the IT department until there is a good opportunity for me to transfer to another department for which I am interested in working.*

mean business ① (of someone) to be seriously determined about what they are doing or to have a strong desire to achieve something ▣ *The research project to develop a substitute for oil is undertaken by three scientists who mean business.*

meet someone face-to-face ① (of someone else) to meet and talk to someone in person ▣ *When I first heard of the death of her mother, I did not want to phone her or meet her face-to-face.*

meet someone halfway ① (of someone else) to reach a compromise with someone ▣ *I have reached an agreement with him after I am willing to meet him halfway.*

meet someone in the flesh ① (of someone else) to see someone in person but they have not seen them in a film or on TV ▣ *Although Jenny said that she was a famous actress, I only met her in the flesh.*

meet someone's eyes ① (of someone else) to look at someone directly who is looking at them ▣ *When Daniel was introduced to me by a friend of his for the first time, I met his eyes.*

meet your match in someone ① (of you) to contest someone who is as good as you or is better than you ▣ *You are preparing for a big tennis match tomorrow. I think that you are going to meet your match in Shirley.*

mend fences ① (of someone) to try improving a difficult relationship that exists between they and someone else ▣ *It is too late for her to mend fences with her ex-husband.*

mend your ways ① (of you) to stop misbehaving and improve your behaviour ▣ *As you have mended your ways, I decide to forgive you and reaccept you as my lover.*

mind your own business ① said by someone to rudely show their refusal to answer a personal question ▣ *"What's your girlfriend's name?" "Mind your own business!"*

miss the boat ① (of someone) to miss an opportunity that gives them an edge over others ▣ *You will surely miss the boat if you do not buy these securities by the close of trading today.*

money talks ① It is used to mean that people with a lot of money gain power and have influence over others and that they can have whatever they want. ▣ *Jessica is a well-to-do woman. As far as she is concerned, money talks, and she can buy this big house if she wishes.*

move in for the kill ① (of someone) to take decisive actions towards their enemy or opponent so as to kill or defeat them, especially when they are already in a weak position ▣ *As our neighbouring country was going to war with another country, our Defence Minister took this opportunity to order the army units to move in for the kill.*

N

neck and neck ① (of two groups or competitors in a contest or race) with an equal chance of winning because they are just as good as each other in terms of their performance ▣ *Our country will go to the poll tomorrow. The latest opinion polls show that the Labor Party and the Democratic party are running neck and neck.*

neither here nor there ① (of something) completely insignificant or irrelevant and not affecting a situation in any aspects ▣ *It is essential that I buy this motor car, and the cost is neither here nor there.*

new blood ① These are the new people, especially the young ones, who are brought into an organisation to introduce new ideas or provide energy. ▣ *The August Ministerial reshuffle gave the Prime Minister the chance to introduce new blood into the cabinet in the hope that this would improve the opinion polls in favour of the government.*

nip something in the bud ① It is used to describe that someone will prevent or stop bad behaviour or a bad situation from happening at the beginning or early phase before it becomes too difficult or unmanageable. ▣ *It is significant to recognise the shoplifting of his nephew and to nip it in the bud before it becomes uncontrollable.*

no holds barred ① without controls, limits, or rules on what someone is permitted to do ▣ *There will be no holds barred in her exclusive televised interview with the prime minister tomorrow night.*

not bat an eyelid ① (of someone) to not show emotional or other reactions that most people would when something unexpected happens ▣ *John's uncle died of heart attack in hospital yesterday night but he did not bat an eyelid.*

not do something for love nor money ① It is used to describe someone either finds it impossible to do something or finds it impossible to persuade someone else to do something. ▣ *He could not solve the crossword puzzles for love nor money.* ② It is used to describe that something is impossible to obtain. ▣ *She could not find her debit cards and credit cards for love nor money.*

not give a toss about something ① (of someone) to not care about something at all ▣ *I do not give a toss about what the teacher thinks about my romantic relationship with a female student.*

not have a clue ① (of someone) to be very bad in a particular activity ▣ *He doesn't have a clue how to talk to people properly.* ② (of someone) to be very stupid ▣ *Peter doesn't have a clue because he can't even solve the most simple mathematical questions.* ③ (of someone) to either know nothing about how to do something or know nothing about how to deal with someone, something, or things ▣ *Mike doesn't have a clue how to toast a cheese sandwich, let alone make a dinner.* ④ (of someone) to not be able to guess, know, or understand anything about something ▣ *He doesn't have a clue where your keys are.*

not have a snowball's chance in hell of doing something ① (of someone) to have no chance at all in doing something successfully ▣ *It seems that Richard does not have a snowball's chance in hell of finishing the project that he is currently undertaking because it has a limited budget.*

not lift a finger ① (of someone) to not make any effort to help someone else or not do something ▣ *John and I visited the old people in the nursing home but he did not lift a finger if I did not ask him to do so.*

not lose any sleep over something ① (of someone) to not worry about something whatsoever ▣ *I really hope to earn a little bit more* *money from investing in the stock market but I do not lose any sleep over this.*

not mince your words ① (of you) to voice your opinion on something clearly and directly, even if you know you will upset people by doing so ▣ *Your teacher Richard told me about your failure in the final school examination and did not mince his words about your poor academic performance in that exam.*

not miss a trick ① (of someone) to know what is happening all the time and take advantage of every situation ▣ *The purchasing manager of our company does not miss a trick whenever there is a bargain.*

not out of the woods ① It is used to mean that there are likely to have more difficulties or to be still in danger before things improve. ▣ *One economist warns that the nation's economy is not out of the woods yet as coronavirus strikes the economy for the second time.*

not pull your punches ① (of you) to speak in an honest and direct way even if it could anger people ▣ *You did not pull your punches and told your lung cancer patient that he would be dead in six months if he did not accept the required treatment as recommended by you.*

not put a foot wrong ① (of someone) to not make any mistakes ▣ *The company continues to employ Jessica because she has not put a foot wrong in her job during the three-month probation period.*

not put your finger on something ① (of you) to not be able to realise, understand, or explain what is different, wrong, unusual, etc. about something ▣ *I could not believe that you could not put your finger on your friend's erratic behaviour.*

not rest on your laurels ① (of you) to be unsatisfied with previous successes and therefore you will try to achieve more successes by doing something new ▣ *I know that you as a restaurant owner will not rest on your laurels because of your intention to open another restaurant in the near future.*

not see eye to eye with someone on something ① (of someone else) to show disagreement with someone about something ▣ *I sometimes do not see eye to eye with my children on what constitutes a good fashion sense.*

not someone's cup of tea ① It is used for describing a particular person or a type of thing that is not of interest to someone or is not liked by someone. ▣ *Going to discos and clubs is not his cup of tea.*

not take no for an answer ① (of someone) to continue trying to make someone else agree with something even after their refusal to agree with it  *Though she disagreed with what I had said, I would not take no for an answer.*

not the be-all and end-all ① not the only thing that is important in a particular situation or someone's life *Failure to pass your mid-term English test is not the be-all and end-all so long as you redouble your efforts to study from now on and pass your final term English examination with flying colours.*

not the sharpest knife in the drawer ① (of someone) not intelligent *I must admit that I am not the sharpest knife in the drawer when I try to solve the IQ puzzles.*

not the sharpest tool in the box ① (of someone) not intelligent *I am afraid that I cannot help you much with your mathematics homework because I am not the sharpest tool in the box when I need to solve complicated mathematics questions.*

O

of the essence ① It is used to describe that something is necessary and very important. *Great brainstorming skills are of the essence to remain innovative in the industry.*

of the old school ① (of someone) with outdated or old-fashioned ideas, qualities, and values *As a designer of the old school, he did not accept the ideas suggested by the designer of our new house to be built next month.*

off beam ① wrong *It seems that my initial cost estimate for painting the whole house is way off beam.*

off the beaten track ① (of a place) isolated and quiet, because it is far from large cities, and so few people will go or live there *The island is sufficiently off the beaten track and as a result, there are very few tourists visiting it even during the holidays.*

off the record ① It is used to mean that someone does not want anyone to report what they have said. *Do not tell anyone what you heard from me because that was off the record.*

off the wall ① (of ideas) strange or unusual in an amusing way *Some of her ideas are just off the wall.*

off your hands ① If someone or something is off your hands, you are not responsible for them any more because another person has taken responsibility for them in lieu of you. ▣ *As my sister has employed a babysitter from Indonesia, who will start working next month, you will take her two children off your hands from sometime next year.*

offer an olive branch to someone ① (of someone else) to shows that they want to come to an agreement with or make peace with someone by what they do or say ▣ *The Prime Minister in Australia offers an olive branch to his counterpart in Israel about exchanging 30 prisoners.*

offer someone a carrot ① (of someone else or a company) to attempt to persuade someone to do something by offering them either an incentive or a reward ▣ *Woolworths is to offer its online customers a carrot this week by not charging them delivery fees for goods purchased from them.*

off-the-cuff ① (of someone) to say something without planning or thinking carefully about it first ▣ *Richard always offends many people by making off-the-cuff remarks.*

old habits die hard ① It is used to say that it is difficult to make people change their ingrained behaviour or attitudes. ▣ *I totally agree with the idiom "old habits die hard", which is used to describe people who are as stubborn as a mule.*

on a knife-edge ① It is used to describe a situation as a difficult or worrying one in which no one knows what will happen next or in which the result is extremely uncertain. ▣ *Whether the economy to recover or not within one year after the COVID-19 pandemic seems to be balanced on a knife-edge at the moment.*

on a shoestring ① (of something done) with a very tight budget ▣ *The wildlife documentary was made on a shoestring.*

on an even keel ① making steady progress, especially after undergoing a period of problems or troubles ▣ *Although the retail store has experienced some financial difficulties at the beginning of this year, it has now got its cashflow back on an even keel after revenue from strong sales resulting from an unexpected influx of customers into the store.*

on automatic pilot ① (of someone) doing something without thinking about it, usually because they have done it time after time before 🔳 *Every Saturday morning, I vacuum the carpet of the whole house on automatic pilot.*

on everyone's lips ① (of something) being talked about by a lot of people 🔳 *The outcome of the presidency election is on everyone's lips.*

on someone's coat-tails ① (of someone else) to benefit undeservedly from the popularity or success of someone 🔳 *Her husband Albert got where he is today on his wife's coat-tails because his wife Susan is a popular actress.*

on someone's part ① done, experienced, or made by someone 🔳 *More hard work on my part could contribute towards the early completion of the project that I am undertaking.*

on someone's watch ① during a period when someone in a position of authority is considered to be responsible for what happens 🔳 *Mistakes were made on my watch, and therefore the decision to quit my job was entirely correct.*

on tap ① (of something) freely available for use whenever needed 🔳 *This encyclopaedia of health provides me with a wealth of knowledge on tap.*

on the hoof ① If someone does something on the hoof, it means that they do something while they are doing something else or moving about, and often not giving their full attention to it. 🔳 *On Mondays, Peter will usually have lunch on the hoof between two long meetings.*

on the horizon ① likely to exist or happen soon 🔳 *There should be a new vaccine on the horizon for treating COVID-19 patients within the next few months.*

on the loose ① (a criminal who has escaped from prison or a dangerous animal that has escaped from a cage) free to move around a place and harm people 🔳 *The dangerous criminal has been on the loose for three years since he escaped from prison.*

on the off-chance ① (of someone) to be full of hope that something good will happen even though it seems unlikely 🔳 *Many tourists has turned up on the off-chance of seeing Prince Charles and shaking his hand.*

on the part of someone ① done, experienced, or made by someone 🔳 *A wrong decision on the part of the government contributes to the spread of coronavirus throughout the entire country.*

on the trot ① (of something happening in a number of times) without stopping in between ▣ *It will be a new record for our bowl club if our team wins another three games on the trot.*

on the up and up ① (of something) getting better all the time ▣ *My friend's career has been on the up and up since he joined our company in 2018.*

on your hands ① If you have a person on your hands, it means that it is either your responsibility to care for them or your responsibility to deal with them. ▣ *You will have the refugee orphans on your hands because you have recently adopted them.* ② If you have either a problem or a task on your hands, it means that you have the responsibility to deal with it. ▣ *You might probably think that it is a waste of time to have this task on your hands, but this is a final step for completing the tax returns.*

one of the boys ① It is a man who gains acceptance by and a sense of belonging to a group of men who behave in ways typical of a masculine. ▣ *He plays basketball, drinks a lot of wine, and generally acts like one of the boys.*

one thing leads to another ① If one thing leads to another, it means that an action or an event will obviously lead to others. ▣ *At first, I was introduced to John at an afternoon birthday party, and later became friends with him because we had a lot in common. We went to the pictures together after the party, but one thing led to another, he ended up asking me out on a date after leaving the cinema.*

one's better half ① one's husband, romantic partner, or wife ▣ *I am glad that you will take your better half to my birthday party.*

one's other half ① one's husband, romantic partner, or wife ▣ *It will be wonderful if your other half can come and meet my wife.*

open a Pandora's box ① to initiate or do something that unintentionally causes a lot of problems previously unknown to you ▣ *The proposal to relax the lockdown resulting from coronavirus outbreak has opened a Pandora's box of arguments among the Labour Government's different factions.*

open season on someone ① when a large number of people are attacking or criticising someone ▣ *At the news conference, it seems to be open season on politicians.*

open someone's eyes to something ① (of someone else or something else) to make someone realise a particular situation or fact that they did not realise before ▣ *The words coming out of Richard's mouth will open her eyes to the fact that the purchasing manager has been receiving the kickbacks for three years from another company in relation to the stationery purchases for our company.*

open the floodgates to something ① (of a decision made or an action taken by someone, a company, or the government) to permit a lot of people to do something that was not previously allowed, or to permit something to happen a lot ▣ *The Australian Prime Minister yesterday decided to open the floodgates to refugees who could stay in Australia so long as they did not commit any crimes before.*

open your heart to someone ① (of you) to disclose your most private feelings or thoughts to someone ▣ *Although Margaret is not your girlfriend, you have known her since you were at primary school. You open your heart to her and so does she.*

OTT ① (of someone's behaviour) exaggerated and extreme ▣ *My close friend was OTT (over the top) with what he said yesterday.*

out of bounds ① (of or part of an area or a place) that someone is not permitted to enter ▣ *The army barracks situated near my home are out of bounds.*

out of nowhere ① very unexpectedly or suddenly ▣ *The Defence Minister told the army to watch out as their enemies could come out of nowhere and attacked them.*

out of pocket ① (of someone) having less money than they begin with after spending it on a project or an activity ▣ *Yesterday I went to the hotel with him to have lunch there. I ended up way out of pocket.*

out of the blue ① unexpectedly ▣ *My uncle living in Canada came to visit us out of the blue.*

out of the top drawer ① (of something) among the best of its kind ▣ *This library is out of the top drawer.* ② (of someone) having had a privileged social background ▣ *Those who travel business class are not necessarily out of the top drawer.* ③ the best people in a particular group ▣ *The landscape gardener that our company outsources is definitely out of the top drawer.*

out of thin air ① (of something happened) quickly and unexpectedly ▣ *A stock market crash normally comes out of thin air.*

out of this world ① extremely impressive or good ▣ *I went to see the play which was great. The music was really good, and the costumes were out of this world.*

out of your hands ① being neither under your control nor your responsibility ▣ *After a babysitter comes, it is out of my hands to look after your two children.*

out on a limb ① (of someone) being alone and in a state of weakness without any support or help ▣ *No council wants to be the first to up council rates. Those councils who have tried to do so will find themselves out on a limb.*

out-and-out ① It is used to emphasise that a person or thing is definitely the particular kind of person or thing mentioned. ▣ *He is an out-and-out conman.*

out-of-pocket ① It is used to describe expenses that someone pays with their own money and that are normally repaid later. ▣ *The out-of-pocket expenses amount to $50 last month. Please repay this to me by the end of next week.*

over the hill ① (of someone) no longer young and so no longer good or useful at doing things ▣ *Do you still think that I am over the hill at 50 years old when I can finish walking up the hills in a few hours without feeling tired?* ② (of someone) no longer young and therefore no longer attractive ▣ *I am over the hill at 60 years old.*

over the long haul ① over a long period of time ▣ *What I think will achieve more for the economy over the long haul are strong leadership, good financial management, prudent economic policy, and patience.*

over the moon ① (of someone) very satisfied or happy ▣ *I was over the moon with the new computer purchased last week.*

over the top ① (of someone's behaviour) exaggerated and extreme ▣ *I thought that the light decorations in the front of our house during the Christmas period was way over the top.*

P

pack a punch ① (of something) to have a very impressive or powerful effect ▣ *This book written by John more than ten years ago still packs a punch.*

pack your bags ① (of you) to leave a place where you have been living or working ▣ *If you can no longer tolerate the high-handed manner of my boss, you should pack your bags immediately.*

paper over the cracks ① (of someone) to hide disagreements, difficulties, or problems ▣ *Although we argue over small matters from time to time, we paper over the cracks by not seeing each other for a couple of days.*

part and parcel of something ① (of something else) an essential and inseparable feature of something ▣ *She is a customer service officer and I am afraid that customer complaints are part and parcel of her job.*

pass muster ① (of something done) to be accepted as good enough for a particular job or purpose ▣ *If the cleanliness of the landlord's house fails to pass muster, no tenants would rent the house.*

pass the buck ① It is an idiom used to describe that someone expects someone else to deal with the responsibility that they have failed to take for the problem caused. ▣ *No one should be tempted to pass the buck to anyone.*

pass the time of day with someone ① (of someone else) to greet someone ▣ *I will always try to pass the day of time with my next-door neighbour whenever I see them while doing my daily Tai-chi exercises in my front garden.* ② (of someone else) to have a short, friendly, and relaxed conversation with someone ▣ *I think it is great to pass the day of time with the people in my neighbourhood.*

past one's sell-by date ① not relevant, not successful, not useful, or not wanted any more ▣ *This type of fitness training is past it sell-by date.*

pastures new ① a new place, job, or activity that opens up many opportunities ▣ *If the company does not promote me within three years, I shall be off to pastures new.*

pave the way for something ① (of a thing or an action) to make it easier or possible for something to happen ▣ *A peace agreement last year paved the way for this week's withdrawal of our troops from this country.*

pay dividends ① (of something done) to bring a lot of benefits in the future ▣ *Taking time out to do exercises every day is time well spent and will pay dividends in the long run as far as health is concerned.*

pay lip service to something ① (of someone or a company) to appear to support or agree with something without doing anything to prove or support it ▣ *This company always pays lip service to career development when it employs new staff.*

pay over the odds ① (of someone) to pay more for something than what it is actually worth ▣ *When I bought this book, I paid over the odds.*

pick up the pieces ① (of someone) to try to make their life normal again after something bad has happened ▣ *Indonesia was struck by an earthquake measuring 6.1 on the Richter Scale yesterday. As there are no more aftershocks today, people are picking up the pieces.*

pick up the slack ① (of someone) to do something, which needs to be done or continued, that someone else is no longer doing ▣ *It was really tough to lose one of our best football players because of his illness. However, a new football player would be employed to pick up the slack.*

pick up the tab ① (of someone) to pay a bill or to pay for a purchase ▣ *Let me pick up the tab for lunch this time, and I will let you do so next time.*

pie in the sky ① It is something good that someone says will happen but that in their view is not likely to happen. ▣ *Ideally, what the general public would like to see is free secondary education for their kids, but I think that is a pie in the sky at the moment.*

play a waiting game ① (of someone) to delay any decision or action because they think that it is a good idea to wait and see how things develop ▣ *I prefer to play a waiting game so that I can have more time to plan what to do next.*

play ball ① (of someone) to do something that someone else wants them to do ▣ *I refuse to play ball if my manager rudely asks me to do a task within an unreasonable time frame.*

play cat and mouse with someone ① It is a situation in which a person who intends to defeat another will find ways and tries to confuse or deceive them. ▣ *The police are playing cat and mouse with the serial killer.*

play for time ① (of someone) to delay until they are ready to do or say something, often by using misleading excuses or unnecessary manoeuvres ▣ *It is quite common to see suspects who are being asked*

play games ① (of someone) to not be serious enough about doing something ▣ *It will be a costly mistake for any company to play games about providing a safe and happy working environment for their employees.* ② (of someone) to treat someone else dishonestly or unfairly so as to get an advantage ▣ *I think it is great to pass the day of time with the people in my neighbourhood.*

play God ① (of someone) to act as if they had absolute power and could do whatever they wish ▣ *Many people fear that scientists and genetic engineers are playing God with nature.*

play into someone's hands ① (of someone else) to act foolishly and mistakenly in the way that their competitor, enemy, or opponent wants them to act with the result that they will have an edge over them or defeat them ▣ *If we swear at the one who has insulted us, we are playing into their hands and giving them the excuse to initiate a fight.*

play it safe ① (of someone) to take no risks ▣ *Play it safe—Avoid undercooking the crab meats. We do not want our guests to get food poisoning.*

play second fiddle to someone ① (of someone else) to have to accept that they are in a lower position of rank or of lesser importance than someone ▣ *Existing employees are not prepared to play second fiddle to new employees.*

play the game ① (of someone) to do things in the way that they have been instructed or in an accepted way so as to retain their job or to achieve success ▣ *If you want to be promoted, you have to play the game.*

play the numbers game ① (of someone) to use figures or amounts in support of an argument so as to confuse or mislead people ▣ *The badly chosen asset valuation method by accountants on valuating certain assets is like playing the numbers game with the purchasers of the assets.*

play with fire ① (of someone) to do something quite risky that could result in dire consequences ▣ *Dating the wrong type of person is like playing with fire.*

point the finger at someone ① (of someone else) to blame someone or say that someone has made mistakes or done something illegal, morally wrong, or unkind ▣ *People should not point the finger at someone just because they do not like them.*

poke your nose into something ① (of you) to become involved in something that has nothing to do with you ▣ *It is better not to poke your nose into other people's business.*

pop the question ① (of someone) to ask someone else to marry them ▣ *Mary is over the moon with her boyfriend Alex because he has finally popped the question.*

pour cold water on something ① (of someone) to criticise someone's else ideas, desire, or plan in such a way that they no longer enthuse about it ▣ *My friends pour cold water on my plans to throw a party for my girlfriend's birthday party next week.*

pour out your heart to someone ① (of you) to disclose your most private feelings or thoughts to someone ▣ *It is very wise of you to pour out your heart to your parents and your wife.*

practise what you preach ① (of you) to do the things that you advise others to do ▣ *You should always practise what you preach.*

prepare the ground for someone ① (of something done or to be done) to make it easier or possible for someone to be successful in doing something ▣ *The notes taken during the class has prepared the ground for me in passing the forthcoming accountancy examinations.*

prepare the ground for something ① (of something done or to be done) to make it easier or possible for something to be achieved or to happen ▣ *Alan's research and analysis prepared the ground for the development of a better computer-based information system.*

press the flesh ① It is a common expression used about politicians, and it means that someone shakes hands with and talks to a lot of people. ▣ *The male celebrity is busy pressing the flesh as soon as his fans come to see him.*

prime the pump ① (of someone or the government) to take action to assist someone else or their business in succeeding or growing, usually by financing ▣ *The government primes the pump to help this well-to-do person establish an online bank so that it can compete with an existing retail bank that has become bigger and stronger over the past few years.*

pull a face ① (of someone) to show their feeling such as disgust or dislike to someone else or something by making some strange facial expressions ▣ *She pulled a face at the unusually strong smell given off* *by the rubber burning outside her house nearby and rushed to open the window.*

pull a rabbit out of the hat ① (of someone) to unexpectedly do something that helps them achieve something, improve a bad situation, or solve a problem ▣ *To be able to sell all 20 trucks to a newly formed courier, the sales manager pulled a rabbit out of the hat.*

pull no punches ① (of someone) to speak in an honest and direct way even if it could anger people ▣ *I had never lied to my uncle in the past. I pulled no punches yesterday telling him that in the Doctor's opinion, his cousin would be dead in a few weeks because of serious illness.*

pull out all the stops ① (of someone, a country, or the government) to make the greatest possible effort to do achieve, accomplish, or do something ▣ *The incumbent government has pulled out all the stops in order to achieve election victory.*

pull strings ① (of someone) to make use of their contacts or influence to gain an advantage, which is an unfair one and an unofficial one, for themself or someone else ▣ *No colleagues liked her because she pulled strings to advance her career.*

pull the plug on something ① (of someone) to stop financing a project or activity so as to force its discontinuation ▣ *Because the country has just gone into recession, the boss decides to pull the plug on this project.*

pull the rug from under someone's feet ① (of someone else) to suddenly stop providing assistance and support to someone ▣ *I couldn't believe that his best friend John pulled the rug from under Adam's feet at the time when Adam needed John's assistance the most.* ② (of someone else) to suddenly take away something on which someone depends to accomplish what they want ▣ *One of the business partners named Peter has decided to pull the rug from under Adam's feet at the last minute by not sticking to his promise of contributing additional capital to help fund the future expansion of the current limited partnership that specialises in dealing with legal matters.*

pull the rug out from under someone's feet ① (of someone else) to suddenly stop providing assistance and support to someone ▣ *Albert is not the one who will pull the rug out from under your feet when you must seek assistance from him.* ② (of someone else) to suddenly take away something on which someone depends to accomplish what they want ▣ *One of the business partners by the name of James has* decided to pull the rug out from under Alex's feet at the last moment by withdrawing his share of capital from the current limited partnership.

pull the strings ① (of someone) to be in total control of other people's action or the events ▣ *I do not know who exactly pulls the strings in this organisation.*

pull your weight ① (of you) to work as hard as other people in a group who are doing the same activity or task ▣ *You are the only person in our sales team not to pull your weight.*

push the boat out for something ① (of someone) to spend a great deal of money on celebrating something or something that they enjoy ▣ *John pushed the boat out for his wife's silver wedding anniversary.*

put a brave face on something ① (of someone) to behave as though a problem or a difficult situation is neither an important one nor a worrying one ▣ *I don't think that Peter is the type of person who will put a brave face on his well-being because he never hides his true feelings.* ② (of someone) to behave as though they are neither afraid nor worried, although they are actually afraid or worried ▣ *Alex is not the type of person who will put a brave face on the announcement of his examination results.* ③ (of someone) to behave as though they are neither disappointed nor upset with a difficult situation because they do not want to let someone else know about how they feel when they are in this situation ▣ *Anna doesn't want her close friends to worry about her so that she will try to put a brave face on her predicament.*

put a damper on something ① (of something) to affect something in a way that makes it less active, enjoyable, or successful than it should be ▣ *Heavy showers put a damper on the outside event.*

put all your eggs in one basket ① (of you) to either direct all your efforts towards or put all your resources into one course of action on which you rely for its only success, but you will risk having no more alternatives should you meet with failure in your initial chosen course of action ▣ *I strongly advise you not to put all your eggs in one basket when you are building an investment portfolio.*

put down a marker ① (of someone) to publicly demonstrate what they are capable of doing or what they intend doing in the future ▣ *The Treasurer has put down a marker about his plans to increase tax for the well-to-do people and reduce tax for the middle-class workers.*

put it in a nutshell ① It is used to mean that someone expresses or says something clearly using as few words as possible. ▣ *I wonder* *whether anyone is willing to give me an update on the matter within ten minutes so that I can put it in a nutshell during the meeting.*

put on a brave face ① (of someone) to behave as though a problem or a difficult situation is neither an important one nor a worrying one ◾ *I suspect that Adam is just putting on a brave face even though he seems to look happy and healthy.* ② (of someone) to behave as though they are neither afraid nor worried, although they are actually afraid or worried ◾ *Alex appears to put on a brave face about the results of the medical examination report that he will find out by this afternoon.* ③ (of someone) to behave as though they are neither disappointed nor upset with a difficult situation because they do not want to let someone else know about how they feel when they are in this situation ◾ *Alex doesn't want his friends to worry about him so he will try to put on a brave face whenever he is in a predicament.*

put paid to something ① (of something happened) to entirely spoil or end someone's plans, chances, or hopes ◾ *Australian swimmers gave a lousy performance here last night that put paid to their chances of reaching the Olympic finals.*

put someone in the picture ① (of someone else or something used) to provide someone with all the information that they need to comprehend the situation ◾ *Please put me in the picture about when the diamonds are sold.*

put someone in their place ① It is used to show someone that they are not as clever or important as they think they are. ◾ *In a few words, the mother put her son in his place, scolding him so hard that he burst out crying.*

put someone on a pedestal ① (of someone else) to consider someone to be perfect, or be extremely talented or good ◾ *I put my brother on a pedestal.*

put someone on the map ① to make a person become famous or important ◾ *The picture that really put this actor on the map was "The missing son."*

put someone on the spot ① (of someone else) to cause embarrassment to someone or to put someone in a difficult situation at that moment ◾ *You have a really bad habit. You always put your friends on the spot so you had better refrain from doing so.*

put someone through their paces ① (of someone else) to get someone to show them how well they perform ▣ *The director of the film put several actors through their paces.*

put something on hold ① (of someone) to decide to do, change, or deal with something later rather than now ▣ *As a result of the onset of the recession, I decide to put the project on hold.*

put something on ice ① (of someone) to decide to do something at a later time than expected, planned, or scheduled ▣ *Albert is putting his plans for a new house on ice until he has found the ideal location to live in.*

put something on the back burner ① (of someone) to defer action on something considered as a low priority at present ▣ *The female architect and builder had to put her plan of building a mansion on the back burner.*

put something on the line ① (of someone) to do something that increases their risk of losing something such as their reputation or their job ▣ *I am not going to put my reputation on the line and take the blame for something that I have not done at all.*

put something on the table ① (of someone) to present something formally to others so that it can be freely and sensibly discussed ▣ *I have decided to put my suggestion on the table.*

put the boot in ① (of someone else) to say very critical or unkind things about someone or something ▣ *It is very cruel to put the boot in the person who is already in a bad situation.*

put the boot into someone ① (of someone else) to say very critical or unkind things about someone ▣ *You should not put the boot into my friends.*

put two and two together ① (of someone) to guess the truth correctly from information that they have about something ▣ *"How did you know Peter was going to tender his resignation?" "I had seen him arguing with his manager on several occasions so I just put two and two together."*

put your best foot forward ① (of you) to work with a great deal of effort and energy to ensure that something that you are involved in is a success ▣ *You must put your best foot forward if you want to become a well-known and reputable builder.*

put your feet up ① (of you) to relax after you have come back from work or after you have done your chores, especially by lying on a comfortable bed or by sitting in an armchair with your feet placed on a footstool ◨ *You should put your feet up after a long day of hard work.*

put your foot down ① (of you) to accelerate your car as soon as you start driving it ◨ *It is a good opportunity to put your foot down because you are the only one driving on this motorway.* ② (of you) to exert your authority to prevent something from happening ◨ *You should have put your foot down when Peter started borrowing your laptop computer without your permission.*

put your foot in it ① (of you) to say something without consideration, and in doing so, you will end up embarrassing or upsetting the person that you are with ◨ *This time you really put your foot in it because you did not realise that it was your friend's mother that you had offended.*

put your head down ① (of you) to sleep ◨ *It is better for you to put your head down at the same time every night whenever possible.*

put your house in order ① (of you) to be sure that you have managed all your affairs properly without any problems popping up at a later stage ◨ *Before handing in or mailing your application form to Centrelink, it is best that you put your house in order by ensuring that you have correctly filled in the required information.* ② (of you) to find all the answers to your own problems ◨ *Please try to get into a good habit of putting your house in order where possible before you ask me to help you solve your own problems instead.* ③ (of you) to improve your own behaviour first before you even consider trying to criticise someone else ◨ *You should put your house in order before you tell me what is right and what is wrong.*

put your money where your mouth is ① (of you) to show either by your actions or by giving money that you support activities or causes that you believe are right ◨ *If something is worthy of your involvement, you can put your money where your mouth is.*

put your own house in order ① (of you) to be sure that you have managed all your affairs properly without any problems popping up at a later stage ◨ *Before handing in or mailing your tax returns to the Australian Taxation Office, you should put your own house in order by checking the figures reported on your tax returns thoroughly.* ② (of you) to find all the answers to your problems ◨ *You should never seek my assistance straight away without even attempting to put your own* *house in order.* ③ (of you) to improve your own behaviour first before you even consider trying to criticise someone else ▣ *You should put your own house in order before you tell me how to behave properly.*

put yourself in someone's shoes　① (of you) to imagine what you would feel like or how you would act like in someone's position ▣ *You will learn to become more sympathetic when you begin to put yourself in other people's shoes.*

Q

quote...unquote　① used at the start and end of a word or phrase that someone else has written or said just to emphasise that they are repeating it exactly ▣ *The cookbook describes this type of avocado as, quote "suitable for salad making and delicious" unquote.*

R

rack your brains　① (of you) to try very hard to remember something ▣ *You racked your brains and you finally could tell me the telephone number of your friend that I also knew.* ② (of you) to try very hard to think of something ▣ *It was obvious that you racked your brains trying to remember the names of your childhood friends with whom you had lost contact.*

raise hell　① (of someone) to behave in a nasty, noisy, or wild way that causes trouble ▣ *Whenever Adam throws a huge party to celebrate his birthday, he is quite worried about the people who gatecrash his party and raise hell while they are there.* ② (of someone) to either complain or protest angrily, bitterly, or loudly about something with a view to persuading other people to improve it or correct it ▣ *Susan will raise hell with whoever she thinks is responsible for the chaos in this suburb.*

raise the ante　① (of someone) to increase their demands or risks in a situation with the purpose of achieving a better result ▣ *The government has decided to raise the ante by not willing to enter into negotiations with the foreign government regarding international import tariffs until a peace agreement is signed between them.* ② (of someone) to offer a higher financial investment or gambling stake ▣ *In order to ensure that Adam will continue to play for our football team, the owner has raised the ante by increasing Adam's existing salary from 2 million* *pounds to 3 million pounds a year because Adam is considered to be one of the best football players in the world.*

raise your eyebrows at something ① (of you) to move your eyebrows upward so as to show that you disapprove of something, you disbelieve something, or you are surprised by something ▣ *At the annual general meeting, I noticed that you had raised your eyebrows at the decision that the retailer would close some of its stores.*

ram something down someone's throat ① (of someone else) to try to force someone against their will to accept, believe, or learn something ▣ *Parents should not ram religion down their child's throat. It should be up to the child to decide for themself whether or not to accept a religion.*

rap someone on the knuckles ① (of someone else) to punish, criticise, or blame someone for something that is considered to be wrong ▣ *His boss rapped him on the knuckles for the failure to finish the project in time for the meeting this morning.*

reach fever pitch ① (of someone) to be extremely excited ▣ *The first goal has caused the crowd to reach fever pitch.*

reach for the stars ① (of someone) to strive very ambitiously for something even though it may be difficult or even though it may not be possible ▣ *Rebecca intends to publish her own dictionary online for the first time. Although she lacks the publishing experience, has a limited range of vocabulary, and is unable to write with a good command of English, she will still try to reach for the stars.*

read between the lines ① (of someone) to attempt to discover, guess, or understand someone else's real feelings, intentions, or meaning from what they write or say, even if they are not stated openly by them ▣ *Reading between the lines, I would say that Mary is very unhappy about the outcome of a court hearing.*

recharge your batteries ① (of you) to regain your energy, liveliness, motivation, or strength by relaxing and resting for a period ▣ *You must be dead on your feet, and you should take a nap to recharge your batteries after spending several hours to vacuum the whole house.*

red tape ① These are the official procedures and rules that appear to be complicated and unnecessary because it is believed to have caused delay in the final result. ▣ *In the past, it was way difficult to get unemployment benefits from the government. The new rules have cut through the red tape to make it easier for the unemployed to get the benefits.*

regular as clockwork ① at exactly the planned times ▣ *I have told my parents that I will make a video call on my laptop computer to them daily regular as clockwork when I shall be in Melbourne on business next Monday.* ② very regularly ▣ *The trams are running regular as clockwork because the new trams have been added to the current tram network.*

reject something out of hand ① (of someone) to reject an idea or a suggestion without both hesitation and prior discussion ▣ *He proposed some suggestions for reducing the company's operating expenses, but the management rejected them out of hand.*

ride roughshod over someone ① (of someone else) to ignore someone's interests or feelings when taking decisions because they are the person in power or in authority ▣ *It is unwise for managers to ride roughshod over their subordinates when they are asking them for a better pay rise.*

ring hollow ① (of a promise, statement, or what someone says or said) to sound insincere or untrue ▣ *What the doctor says about the effectiveness of the new medicine rings hollow.*

ring the changes with something ① (of someone) to make changes to the ways of doing, expressing, or organising something in order to make it more interesting ▣ *When you are making dim sum at home, do ring the changes with its filling by using all sorts of legumes, red meat, poultry, seafood, and vegetables.*

rock the boat ① (of someone) to do or say something that might cause some trouble or disturbances to an existing situation ▣ *He did not want to rock the boat after he had been insulted by a schoolmate.*

root and branch ① (of something) to get rid of something old or traditional and change it permanently and completely ▣ *The new accounting rules will change the way that we report on intangible assets, root and branch.*

rough and ready ① (of something) done hurriedly and imperfectly but good enough for a particular purpose ▣ *Doing an IQ test is only a rough and ready measure of a person's intelligence.*

rough and tumble ① It is a situation in which the people involved compete with one another, often cruelly and do not worry about angering or hurting others. ▣ *Humans often worry about the rough and tumble of public life.*

round the bend ① (of someone) crazy ▣ *He has gone round the bend because he has a tendency to drive so quickly around the roundabout.*

round the clock ① all day and all night with stopping ▣ *In this hospital, doctors and nurses worked very hard round the clock to treat those injured in a plane crash.*

rub salt into the wound ① to cause a difficult situation to become even worse for someone ▣ *Not winning the game was bad enough for me. The fact that I had to put up with insults just rubbed salt into the wound.*

rub shoulders with someone ① (of someone else) to meet and spend time with someone who is usually famous or important ▣ *Commoners rarely have the opportunity to rub shoulders with the royals.*

rub someone's nose in it ① (of someone else) to anger or embarrass someone by reminding them about something they did wrong or failed to do ▣ *People need to break the habit of rubbing someone's nose in it.*

ruffle someone's feathers ① (of someone else) to offend someone by doing or saying something inappropriately or unjustifiably ▣ *I must say that his managerial behaviour does ruffle one of his subordinate's feathers.*

rule the roost ① (of someone) to be the most important and powerful person in a group ▣ *Hou Yifan rules the roost in the Women's World Chess Championship.*

run around like a headless chicken ① (of someone) to be very busy doing plenty of things, but not in a way that is organised and very effective ▣ *When he saw that his home was ravaged by fire, he ran around like a headless chicken.*

run deep ① (of a feeling or problem) be very strong or serious, especially because it has existed for a long time ▣ *The grudge between two employees runs deep.*

run its course ① to develop gradually and finish naturally ▣ *He had no choice but to accept that their relationship had run its course.*

run like clockwork ① (of something) to happen exactly as planned without any difficulties, problems, or trouble ▣ *The concert performance given by this singer ran like clockwork yesterday night.*

run riot ① (of someone) to either act violently or behave uncontrollably ▣ *The parents will have a great responsibility not to let their kids run riot as they are growing up and becoming adults. In order to achieve this, they must start teaching them how to act and behave properly at an early age.* ② (of someone's imagination) to have a lot of exciting, strange, or surprising thought ▣ *His imagination was running riot, considering all the possible ways that he could spend with his recent lottery winnings.*

run the gauntlet ① (of someone) to have to deal with a lot of people who are attacking or criticising them ▣ *At a press conference, the Prime Minister announced to reduce the childcare subsidies for families and he immediately ran the gauntlet of demonstrators.*

run the show ① (of someone) to be in charge or in control of an event, an organisation, or a situation ▣ *The military is running the show to restore order after the recent riot in the country.*

run-of-the-mill ① neither special nor exciting ▣ *He gave an extremely run-of-the-mill speech.*

S

save face ① (of someone or a country) to avoid humiliation or retain respect ▣ *The two countries agreed to reach a compromise after a lengthy discussion in order to save face.*

save someone's blushes ① (of someone else) to avoid doing or saying something that will cause someone to feel awkward or embarrassed ▣ *A guy sent this embarrassing story for publishing in our today's papers yesterday. I saved the sender's blushes by leaving it anonymous.*

save your own skin ① (of you) to try to save yourself from something unpleasant or dangerous ▣ *In the face of a tax office investigation over tax fraud allegation, you are more worried about saving your own skin than preventing your subordinates from losing their jobs due to this serious allegation.*

say something behind someone's back ① (of someone else) to say something unkind and unpleasant about someone to other people without their knowledge and in their absence ▣ *I did not understand why he had said those things behind my back. It appeared that he did not treat me as a close friend.*

say something to someone's face ① (of someone else) to say something, which is often critical, nasty, or unpleasant, without hiding any of their feelings or thoughts in the presence of someone ▣ *No one in the school dares to say nasty things about me to my face.*

scale the heights of something ① (of someone) to be very successful in a type of work ▣ *Alan had already scaled the heights of the accounting profession at the age of 30.* ② (of someone) to rise to a very high position either in the industry that they work in or in the profession that they are in ▣ *Shirley scaled the heights of the accounting industry.*

score brownie points ① (of someone) to earn appreciation or approval for something favourable or good that they have done for someone else ▣ *I thought I could score brownie points with my father by offering to study very hard to get the first place in my class.*

scratch the surface of something ① (of someone) to deal with or experience only a small or a very small part of a problem or subject ▣ *Unfortunately, we have only just scratched the surface of the problem.*

scratch your head ① (of you) to think carefully about a difficult question or problem or to be unsure that what the solution is ▣ *I can see that you are still scratching your heads about which method to use to solve this mathematical equation.*

seal someone's fate ① (of a situation, an action, or an event) to make certain that something nasty or unpleasant will happen to someone ▣ *The head-on collision between the two trucks seals the truck driver's fate.*

see red ① (of someone) to suddenly become very annoyed, upset, or angry because of something that has been done or said ▣ *It made me see red when I saw the bystander who had done nothing to help the poor fellow.*

see someone in the flesh ① (of someone else) to see someone in person but they have not seen them in a film or on TV ▣ *I am very pleased to see Prince Charles in the flesh.*

see someone in their true colours ① (of someone else) to suddenly realise that someone is not as honest or moral as they thought they were ▣ *It was only when John went into partnership with Jessy that he began to see her in her true colours.*

see the error of your ways ① (of you) to admit or realise that you have erred or misbehaved, and are determined to stop behaving badly

It was rather disappointing that it took you so long to see the error of your ways, but it was not too late for you to do so.

see the light ① (of someone) to suddenly understand or agree with something, especially after a long period of ignorance and disagreement *He had been taking traditional medicines to cure his illnesses but he noted that these medicines did not improve his overall health. After rejecting the use of natural medicines for years, he ultimately began to see the light because his overall health had improved as a result.*

see the light of day ① (of something) to become publicly known or available *It is the policy of the government to let the classified documents see the light of day after 30 years.*

sell your soul to the devil ① (of you) to do whatever you need, even if you have to abandon your morals or values, in order to achieve your objective or to get what you want *You should never sell your soul to the devil just because you want to earn easy money.*

send someone packing ① (of someone else) to tell someone in a forceful or in an unsympathetic way to leave a job, place, or position immediately *Sarah has been found stealing stationery from the company. The management has decided to send her packing.*

set alarm bells ringing ① (of something happened) to cause people to become aware of a problem in a particular situation *Thousands of refugees flocked to France and Germany recently because of war in their countries. This set alarm bells ringing.*

set the ball rolling ① (of someone) to begin a process or an activity, which other people will join in with later *One of the big supermarkets has set the ball rolling by cutting down its prices by more than 20 per cent. The other big supermarkets will soon follow suit.*

set the pace ① (of someone) to do something that is considered by other people as a fine example of doing things and therefore they will naturally follow suit *US firms have been setting the pace for artificial intelligence.*

set the record straight ① (of someone) to write or say something so as to ensure that other people understand what the truth really is *I would like to set the record straight on a few points in the project that I am going to undertake.*

set the scene for something ① (of someone) to provide someone else with the necessary details and information so that they can understand what comes next ▣ *The first few minutes of the speech made during the church service was intended to set the scene for the churchgoers.* ② It is used to mean that the conditions have been made ideal or right for something to become likely or highly likely to develop or happen because something else either has happened before or is happening now. ▣ *The poor singing performance of Mary set the scene for the negative feedback from the judges.*

set the stage for something ① to have or prepare the conditions that are right for the beginning or occurrence of something ▣ *The country set the stage for election early next year.*

set warning bells ringing ① (of something happened) to cause people to become aware of a problem in a particular situation ▣ *This country has suffered severe flooding and devastating bush fires this year possibly because of climate change. This will set warning bells ringing round the world.*

set your heart on something ① (of you) to want something so much that you aim at obtaining or achieving ▣ *You seem to love driving very much, and I think it is a good idea to set your heart on a motor car next year.*

set your sights on something ① (of you) to strive to get something that you decide and want ▣ *Although you came from a family of doctors, I think that you still want to set your sights on a career in politics one day.*

settle a score with someone ① (of someone else) to take revenge on someone because of something that they have done to them in the past ▣ *Ten years later, Hamish flew back from United States to Australia to settle a score with someone.*

settle an old score ① (of someone) to take revenge on someone else because of something that they have done to them in the past ▣ *A decade later, Richard is thinking of flying back from France to Australia to settle an old score.*

shoot yourself in the foot ① (of you) to do or say some stupid things which will create problems for you or will harm your chances of success ▣ *Unless you shoot yourself in the foot, you are likely to be elected as chairman of this company.*

shout your head off ① (of you) to shout loudly or rather loudly ▣ *I can hear you shouting your head off among the noisy football crowd.*

sign on the dotted line ① (of someone) to formally agree to something by signing a contract ▣ *You should make sure that you completely understand the terms of this agreement before you sign on the dotted line.*

sign one's own death warrant ① (of one) to behave in a way that will bring oneself disaster, harm, punishment, trouble, or even death ▣ *He signed his own death warrant by crossing the road without paying attention to the traffic both ways.*

sign something's death warrant ① (of something bad happened) to cause the end of something ▣ *The collapse of a large company has signed the entire workforce's death warrant.*

signed and sealed ① (of a document) official and not able to be changed because it is finalised ▣ *This agreement is now signed and sealed.*

sing the praises of someone ① (of someone else) to praise someone enthusiastically ▣ *The English cricket commentator sings the praises of the fastest English bowler.*

sit on the fence ① (of someone) to refuse to say which side of an argument they support or who they support in a conflict ▣ *Both of my friends were arguing and I had decided to sit on the fence by not saying who was right and who was wrong.*

sit on your hands ① (of you) to procrastinate your action when you should be taking it earlier ▣ *You should not sit on your hands when you could see the potential problems with the new accounting system.* ② (of you) to fail to do something that you ought to do ▣ *You cannot afford to sit on your hands because your business is currently experiencing cash flow problems, and you should find ways to cut down on costs in your business as your first step.*

sit tight ① (of someone) to refrain themself from changing their mind or taking action ▣ *His friend Susan advised John not to go the nightclub alone, but he sat tight.* ② (of someone) to stay where they are without changing position or moving away ▣ *Could you sit tight while I ask the doctor to come out immediately to look at your gaping wound on your thigh?*

skin and bone ① (of someone) extremely thin due to serious illness or lack of food ▣ *Many children on the poorest countries are skin and bone due to malnutrition.*

slip on a banana peel ① (of someone) to make an avoidable, embarrassing, or a silly mistake ▣ *He would have won the tennis grand slam if he had not slipped on a banana peel.*

slip on a banana skin ① (of someone) to make an avoidable, embarrassing, or a silly mistake ▣ *The only reason that he slipped on a banana skin on examination day was his poor reading skills.*

slip through the net ① If someone slips through the net, it means that a system has failed to deal with them as it is supposed to do. ▣ *With India's population approaching 1.4 billion, it is obvious that there will be some people who will slip through the net and miss out on receiving their vaccinations.* ② If someone or something slips through the net, it means that a system that was designed to check or assist them has failed to do this. ▣ *This group of people have the responsibility to look for the drug addicts who have slipped through the net.* ③ (of criminals) to avoid being caught by the police on a few or several occasions despite the fact that the police made a few or several attempts to catch them ▣ *The same culprit by the name of Peter, who the police officers believe to have committed the arson, has slipped through the net once again.*

small beer ① It is something that does not seem important when compared with something else. ▣ *The payment for home and contents insurance is small beer indeed when it is compared to the loss of everything due to a hurricane.*

smell a rat ① (of someone) to begin realising or suspecting that something is not as it appears to be or that someone else is acting without honesty in a particular situation ▣ *My boss noticed that an employee in the accounting department worked on Sundays this month. He smelled a rat.*

smooth the way ① (of someone) to make it easier or to make it more likely for something to happen ▣ *All the staff in the purchasing department smooth the way for the newly employed purchasing manager.*

soften the blow ① (of someone) to make something unpleasant seem less unpleasant ▣ *Owing to the fact that the 2 per cent increase in GST was met with strong opposition, the Treasurer tried to soften the blow by upping the tax threshold.*

someone burns their fingers ① (of someone) to suffer the unpleasant consequences of something that they have done but which has gone wrong ▣ *This is the employment agency I tried about a year* *ago but I burned my fingers badly. I would never use the same employment agency again.*

someone gets their fingers burned ① (of someone) to suffer the unpleasant consequences of something that they have done but which has gone wrong ▣ *I once tried this computer shop and I ended up receiving an unworkable computer. I would never go to the same shop again because I got my fingers burned badly.*

someone has a heart of gold ① It is used to mean that someone is generous and kind and enjoys assisting other people. ▣ *Every weekend, he visits a nursing home to help and amuse the elderly people. He has a heart of gold.*

someone has had their day ① (of someone) to be much less popular than before ▣ *Joanna's popularity as a singer has lasted for a few years only. Unfortunately, she has had his day now.*

someone is a dark horse ① It is used to mean that someone does not tell people much about themself and therefore very little is known about themself, even though they have surprising qualities or abilities for achieving success. ▣ *Richard Wong was a dark horse and was not well-known in the field of badminton. He defeated the 2016 badminton championship yesterday.*

someone is a soft touch ① If someone is a soft touch, it means that someone else can easily make them do what they want or agree with them. ▣ *My daughter was a soft touch when I needed to borrow money from her.*

someone is your own flesh and blood ① It is someone who is part of your family, and you must help them when they are in a situation with a lot of problems. ▣ *You are my own flesh and blood. I will stick by you no matter what happens.*

someone lives in an ivory tower ① It is used to mean that someone who has a particular lifestyle or job prevents themself from experiencing the difficulties of the ordinary people with the result that they don't know about their problems at all. ▣ *He lives in an ivory tower. As a result, he is out of touch with most of the community and he does not know the difficulties faced by the poor people.*

someone would love to be a fly on the wall ① said to mean that someone would like to watch what happens and hears what is said without other people knowing that they are present ▣ *I would love to* *be a fly on the wall when my two sisters are having a discussion on when it is best to get married.*

someone wouldn't be seen dead ① (of someone) to say that they would not wear certain clothes, usually because it is embarrassing for them to do so ▣ *He wouldn't be seen dead wearing a pair of trousers like that.*

someone's day are numbered ① (of someone) to be unlikely to remain successful or to survive for much longer ▣ *The drug den is going to be raided by the police, and the drug dealers' day are numbered.*

someone's hands are tied ① It is used to mean that someone is unable to act in the way that they want to because of specific laws, rules, regulations, etc. ▣ *He would like to maximise his business operation overseas but he is left powerless because his hands are tied by the tough regulations imposed overseas.*

someone's right-hand man ① It is someone else who is the most helpful to someone and the most supportive of someone. ▣ *My friend John is always by my side no matter what I do and is definitely my right-hand man.*

something does not come up to scratch ① said to mean that something done by someone is not up to standard ▣ *The athletes in this country are unqualified to compete in the Olympics games if their performance does not come up to scratch.*

something does not hold water ① (of an argument, theory, excuse, etc.) to not seem to be reasonable or true ▣ *The excuse given by an employee for his lateness does not hold water.*

something gets out of hand ① said to mean that a situation becomes uncontrollable ▣ *Two men were arguing outside the nightclub over a girl, but the situation had got out of hand so the nightclub manager had to call the police.*

something has a sting in the tail ① (of a joke, remark, proposal, or story) to contain an unpleasant or a surprising part that only becomes apparent at the end ▣ *You should read the small prints and the written part of any agreement before you sign it, otherwise you will be signing an agreement that has a sting in the tail.*

something has stood the test of time ① (of something) to remain popular, strong, etc. even after a long time ▣ *The classic songs sung by the Beatles have stood the test of time.*

something is close to your heart ① It is used to mean that a subject or something else is of considerable importance to you and that you are interested in. ▣ *I know that there is a special magazine article on improving one's well-being that is close to your heart. I will print this out for you so that you can let your parents have a read.*

something is handed to someone on a plate ① It is used to say that something desirable is given to someone who has not made an effort to get it or has not worked for it. ▣ *No one would be surprised that the presidency was handed to him on a plate.*

something is not up to scratch ① said to mean that something produced by someone or something is not up to standard ▣ *These brands of computers are no longer allowed to be imported from Indonesia into this country as they are not up to scratch.*

something is too close to call ① (of a competition, a match, or an election) to be not possible to have its outcome predicted given that the differences in scores or by the number of votes is very marginal before the end, and the winner can be either way at the end ▣ *The federal election is too close to call at the moment.*

something is up for grabs ① It is used to mean that something is available for anyone who tries to have it. ▣ *Fifty parliament seats are up for grabs in tomorrow's federal election.*

something looks good on paper ① It is used to mean that something looks like a good plan, idea, or argument on the face of it but actually it may not be as good. ▣ *The company's plans to achieve a 10 per cent growth in sales look good on paper only. In actual fact, they are not workable when the country is currently in deep economic recession.*

something rears its head ① (of something unpleasant) to appear or happen ▣ *The bush fire rears its head again this summer.*

something rears its ugly head ① (of something unpleasant) to appear or happen ▣ *The flood of refugees crossing the border into the country has reared its ugly head again this year.*

sound the death knell ① (of something happened) to be the warning sign of the end or failure of something ▣ *The failure of the Republican Party to achieve the majority of electoral votes in the federal election will sound the death knell for this party.*

sour grapes ① a situation in which someone shows disapproval of another person criticises them or accuses them of using unfair methods because their success makes them jealous ▣ *Although our sales team had achieved the first position in sales for this month, the competing teams considered this as sour grapes.*

sow the seeds of something ① (of someone) to either do something or initiate the process that leads to a particular result or situation ▣ *She sowed the seeds of her own success in her retail business by lowering the price of the goods than that of her rivals by at least 20 per cent.*

spare someone's blushes ① (of someone else) to avoid doing or saying something that will cause someone to feel awkward or embarrassed ▣ *I deliberately did not mention his failure in the driver licence test when I met him yesterday just to spare his blushes.*

speak volumes ① If something speaks volumes, it means that something will show either the feelings of a person or the nature of something in a way that is easy to see and understand. ▣ *He says nothing about what has happened to him but the look on his face speaks volumes.*

spill someone's blood ① (of someone else) to injure or kill someone or a group of people ▣ *Owing to his greediness, he spilled his brother's blood in order to take over his newsagent's business.*

spill the beans ① (of someone) to reveal something that was meant to be private or a secret ▣ *In the press conference earlier today, the actress spilled the beans on her affairs with Richard.*

split something down the middle ① (of someone or something) to either divide or separate something into two equal parts ▣ *The Korean War has split the nation down the middle.*

spread like wildfire ① (of a piece of news) to become known by more and more people in a very short time ▣ *Once someone is known to have been infected with coronavirus in a particular suburb, it spreads like wildfire.*

spread your wings ① (of you) to become more ambitious than before by trying to do something that has not been attempted ▣ *I think it is about time for you to leave your old job and spread your wings by becoming a self-published author.*

square the circle ① (of someone) to do something that is either impossible or very difficult ▣ *John squared the circle of making the city of London attractive and sustainable and attracting an influx of tourists from other countries to come and visit the city.*

stab someone in the back ① (of someone else) to do something that betrays and hurts someone ▣ *He decided to stab his housemate in the back because his girlfriend had been cheated by him.*

stand on your own feet ① (of you) to be able to do what you need to do independently without any support or help from others ▣ *You will be able to stand on your own feet if you can find yourself a well-paid job.*

stand on your own two feet ① (of you) to be able to do what you need to do independently without any support or help from others ▣ *If you want to move out of you family home and want to stand on your own two feet, you must find yourself a well-paid job.*

stand shoulder to shoulder with someone ① (of someone) to work together with someone else and support them with a view to achieving a common end ▣ *The US stands shoulder to shoulder with Australia in a determined effort to counter terrorism and violent extremism.*

stand something on its head ① (of something) to make people reach a different or opposite conclusion in spite of the use of the same facts of an argument or a theory ▣ *New evidence has stood the origin of human beings on its head.*

stand up and be counted ① (of someone) to voice an opinion to show their rejection of or support for something publicly, even if doing so might cause them difficulty or harm ▣ *It is time for everyone who is interested in defending the rights to have freedom of speech to stand up and be counted.*

stare something in the face ① (of someone) to have to handle a bad situation that is about to occur, or is highly likely to occur ▣ *If you have stared death in the face, you will realise that life is too short.*

start from scratch ① to start doing something completely new rather than adding something to something that already exists ▣ *The news article is poorly written, and it needs to be started from scratch.*

start the ball rolling ① (of someone) to begin a process or an activity, which other people will join in with later ▣ *We had better start the ball rolling in order to finish the task before the agreed date.*

stay the course ① (of someone) to pursue a difficult activity or task until it has been completed or finished ▣ *The people who are trying to quit smoking should stay the course if they want to be healthy again.*

steal a march on someone ① (of someone else) to gain an edge over someone by doing something before them ▣ *You need to think outside the box if you want to steal a march on your potential competitor.*

steal the show ① (of someone) to get more praise or attention than someone else in a show or other event ▣ *The number one tennis player has stolen the show with his superb performance on the first day of the tennis tournament.*

steer clear of someone ① (of someone else) to avoid someone that appears to be dangerous, difficult, unpleasant, or likely to cause problems ▣ *We should steer clear of the troublemakers or hooligans at all times where possible.*

steer clear of something ① (of someone) to avoid something that appears to be dangerous, difficult, unpleasant, or likely to cause problems ▣ *It is better for you to steer clear of religious or political issues.*

stem the tide of something ① (of an action) to get control of, and place a stop on, something that is unpleasant and is happening on a large scale ▣ *The enactment of the new legislation is meant to stem the tide of drug smuggling.*

step into someone's shoes ① (of someone else) to take over someone's position or job ▣ *It is not easy to find someone to step into Peter's shoes.*

step out of line ① (of someone) to behave unacceptably or badly either by disobeying orders or by violating rules or laws ▣ *The manager warned Alex that he will be given the sack immediately if he continues to step out of line.*

stick to your guns on something ① (of you) to stick to your opinions or decisions despite the fact that other people are trying to tell you that you are wrong ▣ *You should stick to your guns on this issue despite facing a bit of criticism.*

stick your neck out ① (of you) to risk expressing your opinion about something even though other people may not agree with you or you may be wrong ▣ *You will run the risk of sticking your neck out by saying that it might not be necessary to have the annual salary increment this year at the next board meeting.*

stick your nose into something ① (of you) to become involved in something that has nothing to do with you ▣ *Please do not stick your nose into my personal matters.*

stop someone dead in their tracks ① (of someone else or something) to make someone stop doing something or moving because they are very frightened, impressed, or surprised ▣ *The sound of the gunfire in a country being at war with another country stopped most people dead in their tracks.*

stop someone in their tracks ① (of someone else or something) to make someone stop doing something or moving because they are very frightened, impressed, or surprised ▣ *The sound of a gas explosion in a nearby shop stopped me in my tracks.*

stop something dead in its tracks ① (of someone or something else) to make something stop continuing or developing at once ▣ *These job losses could stop Australia's economy recovery dead in its tracks.*

stop something in its tracks ① (of someone or something else) to make something stop continuing or developing at once ▣ *We would need to stop the flooding in its tracks if we were to save the town.*

stop the show ① (of someone) to perform outstandingly in a show or other event ▣ *The female singer stopped the show last night with her beautiful singing.*

strike a blow against something ① (of someone) to do something to damage something to a great degree ▣ *The resignation of the Chief Executive Officer has struck a blow against the company's plans for expansion.*

strike a blow at something ① (of someone) to do something to damage something to a great degree ▣ *The incumbent government's wrong decision to impose a lockdown on the entire country for one whole month seemed to have struck a blow at its chance of re-election.*

strike a blow for something ① (of someone) to do something to defend, help, or support something ▣ *These ten groups of people have recently decided to join force to strike a blow for the freedom of speech and the freedom of thought.*

strike a chord with someone ① (of someone else) to make someone respond in an enthusiastic, an emotional, or a sympathetic way ▣ *The Labor Party's policy on abortion strikes a chord with most young female voters.*

strike home ① (of a situation or what someone says) to be accepted or realised by people, often painfully, that it is real or true ▣ *The harsh reality of losing their love ones during the war really strikes home with the people.*

strike it lucky ① (of someone) to suddenly have a lot of or some good luck that they are not expected to have ▣ *I thought that I would be late for an interview, but I struck it lucky because the interviewer came later than I do.*

strike it rich ① (of someone) to have a lot of money or valuable possessions, especially suddenly or unexpectedly ▣ *My father struck it rich in the mining business.*

strike lucky ① (of someone) to suddenly have a lot of or some good luck that they are not expected to have ▣ *I did not expect myself to win a scratch card yesterday, but I struck lucky and won a prize.*

strut your stuff ① (of you) to show your abilities in a confident and proud way with a view to impressing others ▣ *I know that you are not that kind of person who likes to strut your stuff.*

stuff your face ① (of you) to eat a lot of food ▣ *You must be looking forward to stuffing your face at the banquet tonight.*

sugar the pill ① (of the government or someone) to endeavour to make undesirable news or an unpleasant situation more acceptable to someone ▣ *The government will sugar the pill by offering some financial assistance to those who have been made redundant since the COVID-19 lockdown was initially imposed by the government.*

swallow your pride ① (of you) to be determined to do something and ignore their own feelings of pride ▣ *During the recession, it is better for you to swallow your pride by allying with one of your closest business competitors.*

sweep someone off their feet ① (of someone else) to be so attractive, exciting, or romantic that someone suddenly and strongly falls in love with someone at first sight ▣ *She absolutely swept him off his feet with her gorgeous blue eyes and beautiful round face.*

sweep something under the carpet ① (of someone) to attempt to keep a problem secret instead of dealing with it and hope that it will be overlooked by others ▣ *The treasurer is known to have swept the finance problems under the carpet just to avoid a severe reprimand from the Chief Financial Officer.* ② (of someone) to conceal a problem instead of dealing with it and hope that it will be overlooked by others

There is no point for Alex to sweep the cash-flow problems under the carpet because these problems will continue to haunt him.

sweeten the pill ① (of the government or someone) to endeavour to make undesirable news or an unpleasant situation more acceptable to someone *The lecturer will sweeten the pill by extending the due date of the assignment given to the students.*

T

take a back seat ① (of the first thing) to be given less attention than the second thing because people think that the former is less interesting or less important than the latter *From John's perspective, his own problems will take a back seat to the problems of his family.* ② (of someone) to let other people have all the authority, power, or responsibility *It is wise for Albert to know whether or not to take a back seat in this situation.*

take a dim view of something ① (of someone) to show disapproval of something *I always take a dim view of people smoking indoors.*

take a leaf out of someone's book ① (of someone else) to imitate someone and do something in the same way as them because they want to be like them or to be as successful as they are *He has written a book on how to earns a lot of money in a year. You should take a leaf out of his book.*

take a pop at someone ① (of someone else) to be strongly critical of someone *I cannot resist taking a pop at the police because their incompetence have caused the tragedy.* ② (of someone else) to attack or hit someone *This drunkard is taking a pop at the bouncer.*

take centre stage ① (of someone or something) to be at the centre of attention *I don't like to take centre stage whenever I am on a dance floor.*

take it easy ① (of someone) to relax and not do anything that requires either a lot of energy or too much energy *Peter will have to take it easy this week because he is trying to recover quickly from his headache.* ② (of someone) to relax and neither do too much nor work too hard *I have been told by my wife to take it easy while I am on holidays.*

take its course ① (of something happened) to develop gradually and finish naturally *The real recovery for the tourist industry would not* *come until the countries open their borders after coronavirus takes its course and is under control as well.*

take pot luck ① (of someone) to choose something from what is available with no basic knowledge about it at all and hope by luck it will serve them well ▣ *He hurried to buy a computer from Amazon as he could not resist the bargain offer. In so doing, he just took pot luck.*

take root ① (of a method, a system, an activity, an idea, etc.) to begin to have gained acceptance somewhere by others ▣ *Maoism has taken root in China.* ② (of a plant) to start to grow where someone has planted it ▣ *The new plants will take root in a week's time and they are expected to grow luxuriantly in our garden.*

take second place ① (of a person or thing) to be considered to be not as important as another person or thing and to receive less attention than them ▣ *I would not let my family life take second place to my work life.*

take someone for a ride ① (of someone else) to either cheat or deceive someone ▣ *My sister was taken for a ride two months ago and lost $20,000 as a result.*

take someone under your wing ① (of someone else) to provide protection to someone and be certain that they are all right ▣ *My mother has been very ill recently. I have decided to quit my job in order to look after her at home and take her under my wing.*

take something at face value ① (of someone) to accept what someone else says and believes it without much thought as to its correctness or its truthfulness ▣ *You had better not to take your investment advisor at face value. It is in your interest to get a second opinion if possible.*

take something in hand ① (of someone or the government) to control something with a view to improving them ▣ *It is a bad policy of the incumbent government to only react to events as and when these happen rather than taking the situation in hand.*

take something in your stride ① (of you) to deal with something unpleasant or difficult in a calm, competent, and successful way ▣ *Initially, you had no idea about how to deal with the difficult situation, but your boss had finally helped you take it in your stride.*

take something lying down ① (of someone) to not fight against or complain about a bad treatment ▣ *He criticised me about what I had*

take something on board　① (of someone) to agree to take responsibility for a problem or task and begin dealing with it ▣ *Our supervisor will take your problems on board and will resolve them for you as quickly as possible.* ② (of someone) to accept or understand a fact, a piece of information, a suggestion, or an idea ▣ *Albert took her constructive criticism on board.*

take something on the chin　① (of someone) to accept an event or something that is unpleasant in a brave way without any complaints ▣ *The police arrived to see me wrongly enter the forbidden area in contravention of the lockdown rules. He took the police's criticism on the chin and apologised for the trouble he had caused them.*

take something to heart　① (of someone) to be greatly affected or be very upset by something such as a criticism or warning, or a piece of advice because they think about it seriously ▣ *My boss criticised my job performance from time to time, and I always took the criticism to heart.*

take something with a pinch of salt　① (of someone) to not rely on something such as a piece of information from someone else because they know that they do not always tell them the truth ▣ *The boss has advised all his subordinates not to take the survey results with a pinch of salt. This is because most respondents only provide the answers based on what they feel that they should be giving rather than give the honest answers.* ② (of someone) to not completely believe what someone else has told them because they know that they do not always tell them the truth ▣ *We should take what the young man says with a pinch of salt.*

take somewhere by storm　① (of a drama, movie, play, show, etc.) to be extremely popular or successful in a particular place very quickly, and make a good impression on audiences ▣ *The television drama has taken Australia by storm.*

take the easy way out　① (of someone) to take the easiest course of action, which is not necessarily the best one, in handling a difficult situation ▣ *You should not take the easy way out in this situation because it might not be the best solution to your problem.*

take the edge off something　① (of something else, or something else done by someone else) to lessen the effect or intensity of something on someone ▣ *Many doctors like to prescribe painkillers* *when their patients are in chronic pain. This only takes the edge off the pain but does not cure the disease which causes the pain.*

take the law into your own hands ① (of you) to punish someone who is in contravention of the law even though you have no right to do so because you believe that they have done something wrong ▣ *I strongly advise you not to take the law into your own hands.*

take the mickey out of someone ① (of someone) to laugh at someone else or make jokes about them so as to make them look silly or ridiculous ▣ *He doesn't have the respect for his manager at all because he tends to take the mickey out of him.*

take the plunge ① (of someone) to decide to perform something hard or risky particularly after pondering it for a long time ▣ *She finally decided to take the plunge and become an acrobat.*

take things easy ① (of someone) to relax and not do anything that requires either a lot of energy or too much energy ▣ *John should take things easy whenever he is suffering from stress.* ② (of someone) to relax and neither do too much nor work too hard ▣ *Adam can finally take things easy because it is now his turn to take three weeks of annual leave.*

take to your heels ① (of you) to run away from someone or something quickly ▣ *I noticed that you took to your heels as soon as you saw the creditors who was trying to look for you.*

take up the slack ① (of someone) to do something or to continue doing something that another person is no longer doing ▣ *The basketball team lost some of its best players who had died in a car accident. However, the rest of the team decided to come together and undergo intensive training seven days instead of five days a week. The new basketball players were contracted to take up the slack.*

take your breath away ① It is used to emphasise something is very beautiful, exciting, or surprising. ▣ *I can assure you that the scenery here will take your breath away.*

take your hat off to someone ① (of you) to express admiration for the way that someone has done something ▣ *You take your hat off to a number of your subordinates who support the homeless by preparing evening meals for distribution to them during every weekend.*

tall tales ① the statements or stories that are hard to believe because they are probably not true or highly exaggerated ▣ *She told* *me two tall tales about having met Prince Charles in person and having dined with him.*

teething problems ① These are the small problems that happen in the early stages of a new project, or when a new product becomes available for the first time. ▣ *Comsec upgraded its website yesterday, but it had to take the website offline temporarily because of teething problems that were under rectification.*

tempt fate ① (of someone) to do something that involves unnecessary risks, which may pose serious problems for them or which may bring bad luck to them ▣ *Fire officials said that developers were tempting fate by building houses in the middle of a mountain.*

test the water ① (of a company or the government) to attempt to ascertain what the reaction of the people to a plan or idea might be prior to taking action to make it happen ▣ *The government is testing the water to see what the reaction of the country is to their proposal to cancel the visa of any tourists for committing a very serious crime.*

test the waters ① (of a company or the government) to attempt to ascertain what the reaction of the people to a plan or idea might be prior to taking action to make it happen ▣ *The government is testing the waters to gauge what the reaction of the farmers is to their proposal to increase the farming subsidy for them.*

the acid test ① It is an event or a situation that provides conclusive proof of whether something is effective or ineffective, good or bad, right or wrong, or true or false. ▣ *People are still unsure as to whether the badminton team are up to standard to win in the forthcoming matches. How well they perform in the competition next month will be the acid test.*

the ball is in someone's court ① said to mean that the decision as to what to do next in a particular situation is the responsibility of someone ▣ *I have emailed him about where to buy some fresh and tasty seafood. The ball is in his court now.*

the bare bones of something ① These are the most basic or important facts about or parts of something. ▣ *Just let me know the bare bones of the method.*

the battle lines are drawn ① It is used to say that the opposing groups or people each have a clear and definite idea about the things with which they disagree and they are prepared to start competing with each other. ▣ *The battle lines are drawn between two teams in the school debate. Their conclusions are hotly debated.*

the best of both worlds ① It is a situation in which you gain all the advantages and benefits of two different things without any of the problems or disadvantages. ▣ *The location of my house gets the best of both worlds. The house not only is located in the country but also is close to the Central Business District.*

the big guns ① These are the people who are considered to be the most influential and powerful in an organisation. ▣ *Both Richard and Albert are the big guns who are very capable investment advisors, and they are highly valued by the company.*

the black sheep ① It is someone who differs a lot from the other people in their family or group and who is considered worthless or bad by them. ▣ *All the members of the marketing team in the company are quite capable except for the one who is considered to be the black sheep.*

the black sheep of the family ① It is someone who quite differs from the other people in their family or group and who is considered worthless or bad by them. ▣ *Alex has finished his secondary school recently, and is the only son out the three not actively looking for work. He does not provide for his family and he is considered to be the black sheep of the family.*

the bubble has burst ① A time of great happiness, great success, or great pleasantness has suddenly come to an end. ▣ *The stock market has been rising since 2016. As the share prices are very high and also interest rate is starting to rise, the stock market crashes as a result. The bubble has burst at last, and several million of investors have lost most of their hard-earned savings.*

the buck stops here ① It is used to describe that someone is willing to take responsibility for the problem caused and is not expecting another person to deal with it. ▣ *The buck stops here with the management.*

the buck stops with me ① This is said by you that you are willing to take responsibility for the problem caused and you are not expecting another person to deal with it. ▣ *If the management is going to blame my department as a result of my managerial decisions, the buck stops with me.*

the calm before the storm ① What appears at first to be a false or unnatural period of intense quietness is followed by a crisis or disturbance that one is expecting at a later stage. ▣ *The start of the indoor party was just the calm before the storm, and things had got worse when two uninvited guests came in.*

the common touch ① It is the quality of some people in authority who can understand how ordinary people feel and think and can communicate with them. ▣ *An employee prefers working under a manager who has the common touch.*

the cut and thrust of something ① the aspects of a society or particular activity, which make it challenging and exciting ▣ *My friend enjoys the cut and thrust of tapestry and knitting.*

the dizzy heights of something ① It is either an important or an impressive position of something. ▣ *With his new book release, Anthony has realised the dream of reaching the dizzy heights of fame.*

the dos and don'ts of something ① These are the things that people should do and should not do in a particular situation. ▣ *The author has written a good book that informed the readers about the dos and don'ts of cooking with seafood.*

the dust has settled ① (of a situation) to have become calmer after a massive change, an argument, or a series of chaotic or confusing events ▣ *Now that the dust has settled after my argument with my brother over who is first to get married, we can discuss other matters.*

the end of the road ① It is the point beyond which neither continuation nor survival is possible for someone or something. ▣ *Alex is having a hard time keeping his business afloat and he have come to the realisation that his business may soon reach the end of the road.* ② It is the point where it is no longer possible to go on with an activity or a process. ▣ *I really sympathise with my friend Albert because his marriage has recently reached the end of the road.* ③ It is the unavoidable results stemming from the persistence of the actions of someone. ▣ *If she keeps hanging out with the wrong people, there is only jail at the end of the road.*

the fast track to something ① It is the fastest method of achieving something. ▣ *Doing a few thirty-second bursts of intensive exercise daily is the fast track to a fit body.*

the final straw ① It is the last in a series of difficult or unpleasant events that makes someone feel that they cannot accept a bad situation any more. ▣ *My friend Peter saw someone scratch his new car* *this morning, and it was the final straw for him when his car had been stolen not long after.*

the fine print ① the details of an agreement, legal document, or advertisement that are often printed in very small writing ▣ *Never sign any documents without reading the fine print.*

the game is up ① said to mean that something illegal or wrong that someone has done has been discovered and that they can no longer continue to do it ▣ *The police had surrounded all the possible entrances of the bank and the robber knew the game was up.*

the icing on the cake ① It is something that makes a pleasant activity or situation even better. ▣ *It was my intention to file a lawsuit against my previous employer for sacking me without a valid reason. Meeting John, who worked as a lawyer, at a birthday party yesterday was just the icing on the cake.*

the ins and outs of something ① These are all the complicated or detailed facts of a situation or system. ▣ *I really don't know the ins and outs of the matter.*

the jewel in the crown ① It is the most attractive, the best, or most valuable part of something. ▣ *Alan is the author of a number of books on the English language, and his most recent book is the jewel in the crown.*

the jury is still out on something ① It is used to mean that people have not yet made up their mind about something or have not yet formed an opinion about something. ▣ *The jury is still out on the willingness to take the COVID-19 vaccine.*

the kiss of death ① It is something that certainly ruins a plan or leads to failure in something. ▣ *You had better not to let a new staff take control of the half-finished project as this certainty would be the kiss of death.*

the knives are out for someone ① It is used to mean that people are unfriendly or angry towards someone and they are trying to create problems for them. ▣ *The knives are out for the police officer who has decided not to arrest the shoplifter for stealing on the spot.*

the lesser of two evils ① the lesser of the two unpleasant options between which someone has to choose ▣ *In response to my tough question as to how he would choose between homelessness or sickness. He chooses homelessness as the answer because it is the lesser of two evils.*

the letter of the law ① what is actually written in the law or an agreement rather than the general or intended meaning ▣ *I cannot evict the tenant from the unit now as I need to stick to the letter of the law in the rental contract.*

the life and soul of the party ① It is someone who is fun, lively, entertaining, exciting to be with, and enjoys social gatherings. ▣ *Mary was enjoying very much at a dance party and was clearly the life and soul of the party.*

the light at the end of the tunnel ① It is something that offers hope to someone for the future following the end of a difficult or unpleasant situation that they have been in. ▣ *After the tough past few months, we are finally beginning to see the light at the end of the tunnel.*

the lion's share of something ① It is the largest part or the most of something. ▣ *The Pharmaceutical Benefits Scheme has taken the lion's share of this year's budget.*

the man in the street ① an ordinary person who is a male ▣ *How does the abolition of agricultural subsidies for farmers by the government affect the man in the street and the woman in the street?*

the men in suits ① The men, who are considered as a group and have a lot of authority, manage an organisation or company. ▣ *The board of directors are the men in suits.*

the mind boggles ① It is used to mean that something is hard to understand or imagine because it is very complex, strange, or amazing. ▣ *The mind boggles knowing such extraordinarily big warehouse could be built by Amazon.*

the moral high ground ① It is the belief that someone's actions and policies are morally better than those of their competitors. ▣ *In comparison with the other political parties, the leader of the Labor Party considers that its Party holds the moral high ground.*

the movers and shakers ① These are the people who actively participate in a particular organisation, event, or movement and who often introduce new developments. ▣ *He and his wife have recently joined the Greens Party and have now become the movers and shakers behind the scenes.*

the name of the game ① It is the most significant aspect of a situation or an activity. ▣ *I think that to get a good job, past working experience and qualifications are the name of the game.*

the nooks and crannies ① the less accessible or smaller parts of a place or an object that someone does not normally notice ▣ *After our parents told us that they had hid our Christmas presents somewhere in the house, we began to scour the nooks and crannies for the presents.*

the nuts and bolts of something ① the practical details or facts of something such as a job, a subject, or an activity ▣ *You need to ascertain the nuts and bolts of the projects that you are to undertake before you commit yourself to it.*

the old guard ① It is a group of people in an organisation or society who show resistance to change and whose beliefs and ideas are deeply ingrained. ▣ *The old guard was not re-elected in the AGM held earlier today, and this would make way for a new and more youthful team to take over.*

the order of the day ① what usually happens in a particular occasion or situation ▣ *Wages cut to the public servants is the order of the day in the case of an economic recession in the country.*

the other side of the coin ① It is the contrasting or opposite aspect of a matter or a situation. ▣ *I felt lonely sometimes because I have no friends at all, but the other side of the coin is the complete freedom that I have.*

the pecking order ① It is the social system in which everybody within a group of people knows who has a higher or lower rank than themself. ▣ *The ministers' offices in the ruling Labor Party come in different sizes. The size of the individual office depends on the pecking order.*

the penny drops ① It is used to say that someone finally does understand something that they did not understand before. ▣ *When he told me about the matter, I felt rather confused in the beginning but ultimately the penny dropped.*

the person or thing of someone's dreams ① It is the person or thing that is preferable to all others. ▣ *When I was in Dubai, which was one of the Middle Eastern countries that I toured during last summer, I saw the house of my dreams.*

the rat race ① It is a way of life or job in which people compete aggressively with one other with a view to succeeding. ▣ *No matter where you work, it is the rat race in the workplace.*

the rest is history ① said to mean that everyone knows the rest of the story that someone has been telling ▣ *What happened was that*

Josephine left home because of her husband's affair with another woman and the rest was history.

the rot sets in ① (of a situation) to begin to get worse ▣ *The rot set in when she joined the partnership.*

the sky's the limit ① there is no limit ▣ *His boss tells her to spend some money on buying the Christmas decorations and says that the sky's the limit as to how she can use her imagination in decorating the office.*

the small print ① It is the details of an agreement, legal document, or advertisement that are often printed in very small writing. ▣ *You need to peruse the small print before you sign the rental contract.*

the standard bearer of something ① It is someone who acts as the representative or the leader of a group of people or a particular organisation. ▣ *The fans consider Johnny Wong to be the standard bearer of the football team.*

the state of play ① the present situation ▣ *What is the state of play in the peace talks?*

the villain of the piece ① It is someone who is responsible for all the problems or troubles in a situation. ▣ *The police consider this person to be the villain of the piece for the crime and has decided to tap his phone conversation in order to obtain the required evidence to prosecute him.*

the wheel has come full circle ① to return something, such as an argument, attitude, idea or a situation to its original starting position after a long series of changes or events ▣ *As far as the trend in clothing is concerned, the wheel has come full circle.*

the worse for wear ① (of someone) drunk ▣ *Susan arrived home at dawn, much the worse for wear.* ② (of something) in poor condition due to its frequent use ▣ *After years and years of travelling the rugged terrains for pleasure, my hiking boots were looking the worse for wear.* ③ (of someone) tired due to their great or heavy workload ▣ *Albert comes back home from work today looking the worse for wear.*

the worst of both worlds ① It is a situation in which someone has all the disadvantages and problems of two different things without gaining any of the benefits and advantages. ▣ *The working class got the worst of both worlds: They were out of work due to the lockdown in the country, and they were paying higher prices for groceries due to inflation.*

the writing is on the wall ① These are the clear signs that something will no longer exist or will meet with failure. ▣ *The writing is on the wall, and we only have ourselves to blame if we neglect to do something about it.*

there is little love lost between ① (of two people or groups) to dislike each other ▣ *There was little love lost between the country's two major parties in Australia's politics.*

there is no love lost between ① (of two people or groups) to dislike each other ▣ *There is no love lost between Johnny and his cousin.*

there is no quick fix ① There is no fast and easy solution to the problem. ▣ *There is no quick fix for the development of a completely safe COVID-19 vaccine.*

there's more to something than meets the eye ① said to mean that something is more complicated than it first seems ▣ *There's more to the problem than meets the eye when you consider the scale of it.*

there's no such thing as a free lunch ① said to someone as an emphasis that they cannot get or expect to get something for nothing ▣ *There's no such thing as a free lunch in most cases but there are one or two exceptions.*

there's the rub ① It is used to say that there exists a contradiction or problem that is impossible or difficult to deal with. ▣ *People to whom you are trying to give some good advice think that you are trying to annoy them and there's the rub.*

these four walls ① the room in which someone is having a talk or discussion privately or secretly ▣ *Nobody should be allowed to disclose anything discussed outside these four walls.*

through thick and thin ① in all situations, even if there are difficulties or problems encountered ▣ *Despite my parents showing their objection to the love relationship that I have been having with my boyfriend since 1996, I still love him through thick and thin no matter what happens.*

throw a spanner in the works ① to do something that prevents an activity or a plan from succeeding ▣ *The management's objection to our department's request for the additional funding in relation to the accounting system upgrade will definitely throw a spanner in the works.*

throw caution to the wind ① (of someone) to act either rashly or recklessly ▣ *His friend had thrown caution to the wind by driving so quickly that it almost costed his life.*

throw cold water on something ① (of someone) to criticise someone else's ideas, desire, or plan in such a way that they no longer enthuse about it ▣ *My manager dislikes his subordinate who throws cold water on his management style.*

throw down the gauntlet to someone ① (of someone else) to invite someone to compete or fight with them ▣ *He throws down the gauntlet to the person who wants to start a fight with him.*

throw in the towel ① (of someone) to admit that either they have suffered a defeat or they stop doing something because they will know that they will not succeed while attempting to do it ▣ *It is better for you to throw in the towel if you are sure that you have pursued every avenue in the search for an answer to this problem.*

throw in your lot with someone ① (of you) to decide to work with someone from that time and support them no matter what happens ▣ *I am very delighted to hear that you throw in your lot with my staff.*

throw money at something ① (of someone) to attempt to alleviate or solve something such as a problem by spending a lot of money on it ▣ *There is no point for him to throw money at this problem that is not likely to be resolved.*

throw mud at someone ① (of someone else) to say bad things or spread lies about someone with a view to damaging their reputation ▣ *The three movie stars were very famous, successful, and popular before, but not any more after some people from the film industry threw mud at them.*

throw someone off balance ① (of a piece of news) to suddenly make someone feel confused or surprised ▣ *What threw him off balance was that my brother had been admitted into Cambridge University against his expectation.*

throw your hat into the ring ① (of you) to make an official announcement about your intention that you are going to compete in a competition or an election ▣ *You seem to be ready to throw your hat into the ring for the presidential election early next year.*

throw your weight about ① (of you) to behave aggressively in such a way that you exercise more power or influence over other people than what is necessary ▣ *Stop being a bully and stop throwing your weight about other people!*

throw your weight around ① (of you) to behave aggressively in such a way that you exercise more power or influence over other people than what is necessary ▣ *I demanded that you changed your behaviour and stopped throwing your weight around other people.*

throw your weight behind someone ① (of you) to do whatever is possible to support someone ▣ *I am very glad to hear that you have been throwing your weight behind your husband who is currently running for the president in 2021.*

thumb your nose at someone ① (of you) to show disrespect or contempt for someone ▣ *The judge warned you that he would put you in jail if you continued to thumb your nose at the court.*

tie the knot ① (of two people) to get married ▣ *The couple told their friends that they would tie the knot next year after 10 years together.*

tighten the screw on someone ① (of someone else) to force or threaten someone to do what they want them to do ▣ *The government has started to tighten the screw on companies that try to rig prices or rig financial markets.*

tighten your belt ① (of you) to spend less money than usual because you now have less money than before ▣ *You are burdened with credit card debt because you have a bad habit of spending more than you have earned. From now on, you should tighten your belt.*

tip the balance ① (of a circumstance or an event) to be the deciding factor ▣ *The election promise to reduce taxes for the low-income and middle-income earners helped in tipping the balance in the Labor Party's favour in the last election.*

tip the scales ① (of a circumstance or an event) to be the deciding factor ▣ *The ruling party plans to lower the tax threshold for the low-income and middle-income earners so as to tip the scales in winning the next election more easily.*

to a fault ① more than what is needed or usual ▣ *The poor express their appreciation to him for offering free food and clothes to them and they share the view that he is generous to a fault.*

to a T ① to perfection ▣ *Your bread is steamed to a T.*

to a tee ① to perfection ▣ *The hard-boiled eggs are cooked to a tee.*

to add insult to injury ① to worsen a bad situation by doing something harmful or upsetting to someone who has already been treated badly ▣ *Her girlfriend not only cheated on him, but to add insult to injury, stole his car and wallet.*

to cut a long story short ① to only mention the final point or result of a complicated account of something without providing any further details ▣ *To cut a long story short, she ended up working as a farmer because she loved the countryside.*

to death ① It means "very" when used after adjectives such as bored, frightened, scared, and worried. ▣ *I was scared to death of spiders.*

to die for ① (of something) extremely attractive or extremely good ▣ *Mary, who is my best friend, had hair to die for.* ② (of something) to be desired ▣ *This muffin is to die for.*

to my dying day ① as long as I live ▣ *I will always remember your acts of kindness to my dying day.*

to someone's fingertips ① in every way ▣ *He is Italian to his fingertips.*

to the core ① in every way ▣ *He is a capitalist to the core.* ② to the greatest degree possible ▣ *I was upset to the core after hearing the death of my work colleague.*

to the hilt ① (of something done by someone) as much as possible ▣ *They will fight for freedom of speech to the hilt.*

toe the line ① (of someone) to behave in a way that is expected of them by the people who are in a position of authority or who are in charge, whether they agree with them or not ▣ *Employees who will not toe the line are given either a warning or the sack.*

tongue in cheek ① (of a piece of writing or a remark) being meant to be ironically funny and not taken seriously ▣ *Her comments about the Peter's love affair with Susan were tongue in cheek.*

touch a nerve ① (of someone) to anger or embarrass someone else by mentioning something that they are very sensitive about or feel strongly about ▣ *He touched a nerve when he said nasty things about his friend's parents.*

touch a raw nerve ① (of someone) to anger or embarrass someone else by mentioning something that they are very sensitive about or feel strongly about ▣ *People could have avoided touching a raw nerve if* *they had put some thought into what words should come out of their mouths.*

touch wood   ① said after someone has had a run of good luck in the past, in order to avoid bad luck and have good luck in the future ▣ *My son is going to pass the economic examination, touch wood.*

tread on someone's toes   ① (of someone else) to offend someone by what they do or say, especially by involving themself in matters that are someone's responsibilities ▣ *I hope that she will not tread on his toes when she will see him this afternoon.*

tread water   ① (of someone) to make no headway in the particular situation but just to continue doing the same thing ▣ *We are still treading water at the present moment, but we hope the other company will sign the business deal with our company soon.*

try your hand at something   ① (of you) to try doing something that you have not tried previously ▣ *Will you try your hand at poetry?*

tug at the heartstrings   ① (of something such as a ballad, film, poem, music, speech, song, story, or video) to cause someone to have strong feelings of love, pity, or sympathy ▣ *This ballad is guaranteed to tug at the heartstrings.*

turn a blind eye to something   ① (of someone) to deliberately ignore something that they know about by not taking the appropriate action that they should be taking in the first place ▣ *The teacher turned a blind eye to one of his students who had cheated in the school examination.*

turn heads   ① (of someone or something) to be so unusual, beautiful, or impressive that it will attract a great deal of attention from people once they see them ▣ *Josephine turned heads when she had arrived at the dance party.*

turn in one's grave   ① It is used to mean that the deceased would disapprove of something that is happening now if they were aware of it. ▣ *Selling this house immediately after the death of my great-grandfather instead of a few years later would have him turning in his grave.*

turn over a new leaf   ① (of someone) to change the way that they behave to become a better person or a more acceptable person ▣ *I see adulthood as a chance to turn over a new leaf.*

turn something on its head   ① (of someone) to make someone else reach a different or opposite conclusion in spite of the use of the same facts of an argument or a theory ▣ *Instead of requesting the inclusion of this medicine for the stomach cancer in the Pharmaceutical Benefits Scheme, we should turn the argument on its head and point out the cost of health care in relation to the illness.*

turn the other cheek　① (of someone) to take no action against someone else when someone has been attacked or insulted by them ▣ *Although we argued heatedly with each other over this matter, neither of us would turn the other cheek.*

turn the screw on someone　① (of someone else) to force someone to do what they want by intimidating them ▣ *The captors have the habit of turning the screw on their captives who do not listen to them.*

turn the tables on someone　① (of someone else) to do something to reverse their situation to that of someone in a way that someone else now has the advantage over someone who previously had the edge over someone else ▣ *He turned the tables on his rival with allegations of unfair business practices.*

turn up the heat on someone　① (of someone else) to force or persuade someone to do something against their will ▣ *Our supermarket ups its sales by turning up the heat on its competitors through a 30% price reduction in our goods sold to the consumers. This may result in our rival supermarkets running at a loss.*

turn up your nose at something　① (of you) to refuse to accept something because in your opinion it is not good enough ▣ *Are you one of the university graduates who tend to turn up your nose at government jobs and try to look for business jobs instead?*

turn your back on someone　① (of you) to ignore, leave, or reject someone ▣ *You should try not to turn your back on the needy or the poor when they ask for your help.*

turn your back on something　① (of you) to ignore, leave, or reject something ▣ *Given that you are the incumbent Tourism Minister, your decisions will have a great impact on the tourism industry, and therefore you cannot afford to turn your back on the issues of domestic and international tourism.*

turn your hand to something　① (of you) to do something well even if you may not be trained to do it or it is your first time doing it ▣ *You are likely to turn your hand to most house chores than most people.*

under a cloud ① It is used to describe that someone is criticised or disapproved of because they have done something wrong or because they have come under suspicion. ▣ *One of the employees called John has recently resigned under a cloud after he is alleged to have embezzled $300,000.*

under false pretences ① If someone does something under false pretences, they do it by tricking others, or by not telling the truth about either themself or their intentions. ▣ *He admitted that he had brought her here under false pretences.*

under par ① not up to the expected standard ▣ *His tennis performance is under par this year.*

under sail ① It is used for describing someone who is travelling in either a boat or a ship that has sails. ▣ *After 38 days under sail, we reached the coastline of United Kingdom.*

under the weather ① (of someone) not feeling well ▣ *I did not go to work yesterday because I was under the weather.*

under your nose ① It is used for describing something bad or something illegal that happens either in front of you or very close to you, and that there is nothing you can do to stop it. ▣ *There is no doubt that someone in this company is stealing stationery right under your nose.*

until my dying day ① as long as I live ▣ *I will not move out of my mansion until my dying day.*

up and running ① (especially of a machine or system) functioning or working successfully after a good start ▣ *For the new trains to be up and running at all times after their initial trial use, we must invest heavily in both the people and technology.*

up in the air ① (of a plan) not yet decided ▣ *At the present moment, the plan to expand our company is still up in the air.*

up the ante ① (of someone) to increase their demands or risks in a situation with the purpose of achieving a better result ▣ *The foreign government wants to up the ante by refusing to negotiate with our government regarding international trade until a peace treaty is formally drawn up and signed.* ② (of someone) to offer a higher financial investment or gambling stake ▣ *With a view to ensuring that*

Albert will keep playing for our cricket team, the owner has upped the ante by raising Albert's current salary from 2 million pounds to a staggering 5 million pounds a year because Albert is viewed as one of the top cricket players in the world.

up to the hilt ① (of something done by someone) as much as possible ▣ *We should support you up to the hilt.*

V

vanish into thin air ① (of someone or something) to suddenly and completely disappear ▣ *Our daughter vanished into thin air ten years ago and all hopes of finding her alive have vanished.*

vote with your feet ① (of you) to show your desire or to express your opinion through your actions such as by deciding not to spend money at a place ▣ *I think that you will vote with your feet after hearing from your friends that the new store has been charging ridiculous prices for any products sold to their customers.* ② (of you) to show your desire or to express your opinion through your actions such as by leaving or not going to a place ▣ *When the price of paragliding trebled last month, you voted with your feet and just decided not to go.*

W

wait in the wings ① (of someone) to take action when there is a window of opportunity available ▣ *Several staff in different departments are waiting in the wings for their promotion to junior managers.*

walk a tightrope ① (of someone) to have to deal with a difficult situation where they have to be very careful in what they say or do, especially one involving an attempt to satisfy opposing groups or making a decision between the opposing plans or actions ▣ *John is walking a tightrope between the mature politicians and immature politicians within the Labor Party.*

walk into the lion's den ① (of someone) to intentionally place themself in a dangerous or tough situation ▣ *Josephine dressed herself in a school uniform and later walked in the garden so as to lure and catch the serial rapist. She really walked into the lion's den.*

warts and all ① It is a description or inclusion of all the qualities or features that are neither attractive nor appealing in a person's character. ▣ *I shall be married to this person, warts and all.*

wash your dirty linen in public ① (of you) to discuss something embarrassing, bad, or unpleasant publicly, which should have been kept private ▣ *You should not wash your dirty linen in public.*

wash your hands of something ① (of you) to no longer accept responsibility for a problem ▣ *You should not wash your hands of responsibility for the flagging economy. Instead, you should apologise to the people in this case and take appropriate action to boost the economy.* ② (of you) to say that you will not take part in something ▣ *I think you have made the right decision to wash your hands of this sordid business.*

weather the storm ① (of a company or someone) to manage to get to the end of a very difficult situation without being harmed or being affected by it in a very bad way, or without being adversely affected by it in any way at all ▣ *The company weathered the storm of a takeover attempt by its largest competitor.* ② (of someone) to manage to solve a very difficult problem ▣ *We shall see if his manager can weather the storm caused by the actions of his subordinates.*

welcome someone with open arms ① (of someone else) to show someone that they are very happy to see them ▣ *I welcomed my wonderful parents with open arms.*

What planet does someone come from? ① It is said humorously to point out that someone has ideas that are crazy, impractical, or not sensible. ▣ *He thinks that monkeys are more intelligent than human beings. What planet does he come from?*

What planet is someone on? ① It is said humorously to point out that someone has ideas that are crazy, impractical, or not sensible. ▣ *He prefers raw meat to cooked meat. What planet is he on?*

when it comes to the crunch ① when a very difficult or important point is reached or when an event occurs to the extent that someone must take decisive action immediately ▣ *When it comes to the crunch, I will discontinue the project, thereby avoiding the demise of the company.*

when push comes to shove ① when a situation reaches a crucial point, someone must make a decision on how to continue ▣ *When push* *comes to shove, I know that I need to devise an alternative plan to go forward.*

when the chips are down ① It is used to describe that someone is in either a very dangerous situation or a very difficult situation and is forced to decide what is important to them. ▣ *When the chips are down, you must have a clear head if you were to make the right decision.*

whet someone's appetite for something ① (of a circumstance or situation) to give someone a small experience of something so as to increase their interest in and desire for it ▣ *The fact that our basketball team have defeated their competing team this morning do not whet their appetite for more intensive training that is required of them if they want to achieve even greater success in the future.*

whip something into shape ① (of someone) to use whatever methods that are needed to change or ameliorate something in order to make it reach the required standard ▣ *An experienced university professor could whip any of his students who had been performing poorly into shape.*

wide of the mark ① neither correct nor accurate ▣ *It is highly likely that the figures shown on this financial report are wide of the mark.*

win brownie points ① (of someone) to earn appreciation or approval for something favourable or good that they have done for someone else ▣ *He is not doing anything more than required of him just to win brownie points.*

win something hands down ① (of someone) to win something such a contest or a prize with ease ▣ *Alan won the Ping-Pong Men's Final hands down.*

wipe the slate clean ① (of someone) to agree to not remember about something such as arguments or mistakes that happened in the past ▣ *They agreed to wipe the slate clean and became good friends again.*

wish you could turn back the clock ① (of a person) to wish you can return to a situation that used to exist because the current one is unpleasant ▣ *I wish you could turn back the clock and did not do such a nasty thing to me.*

with a capital ... ① to give emphasis to the word that has a particular significance in the situation that someone is referring to or talking about ▣ *My parents are healthy with a capital H.*

with an iron fist ① with the use of great force and often with violence ▣ *The Normans conquered the English with an iron fist in 1066.*

with bated breath ① It is used to describe someone who feels anxiously and excitedly and is waiting to see what will happen next. ▣ *I waited for the English examination results with bated breath.*

with flying colours ① very successfully ▣ *He was able to pass his accountancy examination with flying colours.*

with no strings attached ① (of an agreement, or an offer) with no restrictions applied to it or with no special conditions attached to it ▣ *The home and contents insurance policy offered 5% discount for seniors with no strings attached.* ② (of a form of assistance that has been provided or will be provided by someone to someone else) with no expectation of anything in return from someone else ▣ *Shirley will help Alan financially with no strings attached.*

with the greatest of ease ① very easily ▣ *This computer system can be assembled with the greatest of ease.*

with the naked eye ① with only the eyes and without the assistance of a pair of glasses, a telescope, a microscope, etc. ▣ *Most bacteria are just too small to be seen with the naked eye.*

with your bare hands ① without the use of any tools or weapons ▣ *You are very brave because you have managed to knock down the armed thief with your bare hands.*

within limits ① within something such as a level, a time frame, an amount, or the time that is considered allowable or reasonable ▣ *I will pay for your credit card debts - within limits.*

within spitting distance of something ① very close to something ▣ *He lives within spitting distance of the bakery.*

within striking distance of something ① close to something ▣ *Their family lives within striking distance of both Blacktown and Seven Hills.* ② near enough to attack something with ease ▣ *The fierce looking tiger was now within striking distance of its prey.* ③ very close to achieving or getting something ▣ *Being in the 2021 Australian Open Men's Singles Final puts me within striking distance of a tennis grand slam.*

worth someone's salt ① (of someone) to deserve respect or to do their job well ▣ *Any accountant worth their salt would be very familiar with the accounting procedures and standards.*

wring your hands ① (of you) to express that you are worried or upset about something unpleasant by rubbing or twisting your hands ▣ *I noticed that you were wringing your hands over the unresolved pay dispute.*

your bread and butter ① It is an activity or a job that provides you with the main source of income on which you live. ▣ *It seems that landscaping is your bread and butter at the moment.*

A

A bad excuse is better than none. ① It is better to give a poor or an implausible excuse for an unwanted action than to offer no explanation at all.

A bad penny always turns up. ① A person or thing that is unwanted or unpleasant tends to appear or reappear, especially at inopportune times.

A bad tree does not yield good apples. ① Bad parents do not bring up good children.

A bad workman blames his tools. ① In the case of bad workmanship, a workman tends to lay the blame on his equipment when in actual fact he lacks the necessary skills to complete his job.

A barking dog seldom bites. ① Don't be afraid of people who threaten you or say that they will do something bad to you since they often do not take actions to harm you.

A bird in hand is worth two in a bush. ① The things we already have are more valuable than trying to get something better that may come to nothing.

A black plum is as sweet as a white. ① Don't judge people by their external appearance.

A book holds a house of gold. ① There is a wealth of knowledge in books. For example, adults use the Chinese proverbs to encourage youngsters to study. If they study hard, good things will come to them such as a good job as well as a chance to make good money.

A broken friendship may be soldered but it will never be sound.
① A friendship can be re-established after an argument but will never be as strong as before.

A broken friendship may be soldered but will never be sound.
① A friendship can be re-established after an argument but will never be as sound as before.

A burden of one's own choice is not felt. ① Something hard appears to be easier when it is done of one's own accord.

A burnt child dreads the fire. ① A bad or an undesirable experience will make people avoid certain things.

A calm sea does not make a skilled sailor. ① A person shows their competencies or abilities when the challenging experiences or difficulties arise.

A cat has nine lives. ① Cats can survive many accidents because they land on their feet without harming themselves.

A chain is no stronger than its weakest link. ① The strength of a group relies upon each individual member in the entire group.

A change is as good as a rest. ① Doing something different from one's routine is often as refreshing as taking a break or holiday.

A closed mouth catches no flies. ① It is better to stay silent than to talk so as to avoid getting into troubles.

A constant guest is never welcome. ① If you visit your friends occasionally, you are very welcome. On the other hand, if you visit them too often, they have the tendency to grow to dislike you.

A danger foreseen is half avoided. ① If you anticipate having problems or difficulties in doing a job, it will be easier to tackle.

A day of sorrow is longer than a month of joy. ① Time goes very fast when you are happy than when you are sad.

A drop of ink may make a million think. ① A thought expressed in writing (perhaps published in a newspaper) can exert an influence over a large number of people.

A dry March, a wet April and a cool May may fill barn and cellar and bring much hay. ① Harvest predictions are made according to the weather.

A fault confessed is half redressed. ① Confession is the start of forgiveness.

A flower blooms more than once. ① If you miss an opportunity to do something, you can make use of another one at a later time.

A fly will not get into a closed mouth. ① If you know when to keep silent, you will not run into trouble.

A fool and his money are easily parted. ① A stupid or foolish person usually spends money carelessly.

A fool and his money are soon parted. ① A stupid or foolish person usually spends money carelessly.

A fool at forty is a fool forever. ① If a person has not started to behave sensibly and reasonably by the time that they reach forty, they never will.

A friend in need is a friend indeed. ① A real friend is a friend who helps you when you face difficulties.

A friend to all is a friend to none. ① If everyone is your friend to the same degree, then friendship is not something unique.

A friend's eye is a good mirror. ① We can trust our friend to tell us the truth.

A good beginning makes a good end. ① Plan a task carefully and there is a better chance of getting it done well.

A good conscience is a soft pillow. ① You can sleep well if there is nothing that you feel guilty about.

A good example is the best sermon. ① Providing a good example is better than just offering advice.

A good mind possesses a kingdom. ① Intellectual assets are more precious than material ones.

A good name is better than a good face. ① Having a good reputation is better than having good looks.

A growing youth has a wolf in his belly. ① A young person who is growing fast and hungry all the time eats a lot as a result.

A guilty conscience needs no accuser. ① If you have done something wrong and feel guilty about it, you will feel uncomfortable and want to confess even if no one accuses you of wrongdoing.

A handful of patience is worth more than a bushel of brains. ① Having patience is considered to be more precious than having intelligence.

A happy heart is better than a full purse. ① Being happy is better than possessing wealth.

A heavy purse gives to a light heart. ① What makes you feel more cheerful and secure is when you have plenty of money.

A hedge between keeps friendship green. ① Friendship will last a long time so long as friends respect each other's privacy.

A hungry belly has no ears. ① A hungry person is unable to concentrate on or is not interested in anything else other than to eat.

A hungry wolf is fixed to no place. ① A desperate person will go to different places one after the other when they need to meet their needs.

A leopard cannot change its spots. ① A person cannot change their character or personality no matter how hard they try.

A lie begets a lie. ① Once you tell a lie, you will end up telling another one.

A little fire is quickly trodden out. ① If you deal with a small problem quickly, it will be easily solved and will not become a major issue.

A loaded wagon makes no noise. ① Bragging is not something someone becomes involved in if they are of good character or personality.

A loveless life is a living death. ① Life is hard without love.

A man is as old as he feels himself to be. ① It does not matter how old a man looks as long as he stays well and healthy.

A man is judged by his deeds, not by his words. ① A person is judged by their action or performance but is not judged by what they say that they will do.

A man is known by the company he keeps. ① A person's personality is judged by the kinds of people with whom they spend their time.

A monkey in silk is a monkey no less. ① It does not matter how a person dresses because they are the same person underneath.

A new broom sweeps clean. ① Someone with a new perspective can make great changes fast.

A nod is as good as a wink to a blind horse. ① A suggestion or a hint is good enough for someone to understand without the need for further explanation or elaboration.

A picture paints a thousand words. ① A picture can express a complex and sometimes multiple ideas in the same manner that a large amount of descriptive text can.

A problem shared is a problem halved. ① If you tell someone about a problem, it is easier to handle.

A rising tide lifts all boats. ① When an economy is performing well, all people will benefit from it.

A rolling stone gathers no moss. ① If a person continues to move from one place to another, they gain neither friends nor possessions.

A rotten apple spoils the barrel. ① Someone who is dishonest or immoral can have adverse influence on the entire group.

A smooth sea never made a skilled mariner. ① Overcoming trouble or difficulty will allow one to gain new competence.

A soft answer turns away wrath. ① A polite or gentle reply to someone who is angry will calm them.

A stitch in time saves nine. ① If you sort out a problem at an early stage, you will save time and extra work later.

A stumble may prevent a fall. ① Rectifying a minor mistake may help you avoid making a bigger mistake.

A swallow does not make the summer. ① One day or a short time of happiness does not make a person completely happy.

A tidy house holds a bored woman. ① The woman who is the owner of the house will have nothing to occupy her time if the house is always clean and is in good order.

A tree is known by its fruit. ① A person is judged by how they act.

A watched pot never boils. ① What seems to take a long time for something to happen is when you have waited anxiously.

A wise head keeps a still tongue. ① A person of intelligence or wisdom will know when not to say a thing or when to stop talking.

A wonder lasts but nine days. ① Life will go on like before despite the fact that an event that initially attracts a lot of attention for only a short time will soon be forgotten by the people.

A worry shared is a worry halved. ① It is easier for you to handle a problem if you tell someone about it.

A young idler, an old beggar. ① If you want to have money when you are old, it is important to work hard when you are young.

Absence makes the heart grow fonder. ① You will have more love for the people whom you love when they are away from you.

Accidents will happen. ① Some unfortunate events must be accepted as unavoidable.

Actions speak louder than words. ① A person's actions are a better indication of their character than what they say.

Adversity makes strange bedfellows. ① Difficult circumstances and times of trouble often bring people together and cause them to form alliances.

Advice is cheap. ① Giving somebody some advice does not involve any cost.

Advice is least heeded when most needed. ① Advice is something that wise men don't need and foolish people won't take and the greater the need for advice, the less likely the foolish person is to heed it.

Advisers run no risks. ① To offer advice is easier than to act.

After dinner rest a while, after supper walk a while. ① Dinner is called 'lunch' nowadays, and supper has become 'dinner'.

Age before beauty. ① Older people should be given precedence over younger people.

Agree, for the law is costly. ① It is wise to reach a compromise instead of pursuing an expensive lawsuit.

All cats are grey in the dark. ① Physical appearance is unimportant when it is dark.

All covet, all lose. ① If you endeavour to avoid everything, you run the risk of losing everything.

All days are short to industry and long to idleness. ① Time passes slowly when there is nothing for you to do.

All good things come to those who wait. ① If you are persistent and patient, you will ultimately achieve your goals.

All in good time. ① Be patient as the things will happen at the opportune time.

All is fair in love and war. ① You do not have to abide by the usual rules about what constitutes reasonable behaviour in love and war.

All roads lead to Rome. ① There are many different methods or ideas to reach the same outcome.

All that glitters is not gold. ① What appears to be superficially good but it might not be so when you look at it more closely.

All things are difficult before they are easy. ① If you practise, everything becomes much easier.

All things grow with time - except grief. ① As time passes, sadness will gradually reduce.

All work and no play makes Jack a dull boy. ① All good things come to an end. Nothing lasts forever.

All's well that ends well. ① A person can forget about how unpleasant or difficult something was because everything ends in satisfaction.

An ant may well destroy a whole dam. ① A small problem can sometimes cause a lot of damages.

An apple a day keeps the doctor away. ① Eating nutritious food will make you healthier and as a result, you don't have to go to the doctor very often.

An empty purse frightens away friends. ① Your friends tend to disappear when your financial situation turns bad or deteriorates.

An Englishman's home is his castle. ① An Englishman's home is a place where he feels secure, enjoys privacy, and can do whatever he wishes.

An idle brain is the devil's workshop. ① You can avoid temptation when you are busy working on something or working all the time.

An old fox is not easily snared. ① A person with years of experience is unlikely to be fooled.

An onion a day keeps everyone away. ① A humorous version of "an apple a day keeps the doctor away".

An ounce of discretion is worth a pound of wit. ① It is better to speak in a careful and polite way rather than to make jokes or remarks that others might find offensive.

An ounce of prevention is worth a pound of cure. ① It is wiser and easier to prevent a problem, illness, etc. from happening than to stop or correct it after its occurrence.

Anger is the one thing made better by delay. ① When you are angry, it will do you good not to speak or act right away.

Another day, another dollar. ① A job may be boring or difficult but the only benefit is a small amount of payment after the completion of the job.

Any time means no time. ① If the date of an event remains unspecified, it will never happen.

April showers bring May flowers. ① A period of discomfort now can form the basis of a period of happiness and joy in the future.

As you sow, so shall you reap. ① You have to accept the outcomes of your actions.

Ask me no questions, I'll tell you no lies. ① Don't ask me the questions if you think that you will not like the answer.

B

Bad news travels fast. ① News relating to misfortune, accidents, illness, trouble, etc. circulates quickly.

Be just before you are generous. ① Make sure all your debts are paid before you begin to offer help to others.

Be swift to hear, slow to speak. ① Listen carefully prior to speaking.

Beauty is in the eye of the beholder. ① Not everyone will have the same opinions about what is attractive.

Beauty is only skin-deep. ① External attractiveness is not indicative of a person who has a good or an essential personality.

Better an egg today than a hen tomorrow. ① It is better to have a sure thing now than to know that there is a possibility of having more of it later.

Better be alone than in bad company. ① It is better to be alone than to have friends with a bad personality and character.

Better be the head of a dog than the tail of a lion. ① It is wiser to be the head of a small group that is not very important than that of a bigger one that is important.

Better be untaught than ill-taught. ① It is better not to learn from a bad teacher at all because they will teach you badly.

Better flatter a fool than fight him. ① It is wise to avoid arguments with silly or foolish people.

Better late than never. ① It is better to do something after the expected time than not to do it at all.

Better lose the saddle than the horse. ① It is better to take a small loss than to continue and jeopardise losing everything.

Better safe than sorry. ① It is wise for you to be careful in doing something by not acting hastily. As a result, you will avoid doing something that you may regret later.

Better the devil you know than the devil you don't know. ① It is wise for you to deal with a familiar situation even though you might sometimes find it undesirable, and it would be foolish for you to risk a change that might make the situation worse.

Better to drink the milk than to eat the cow. ① Be careful not to ruin the source of your welfare or income.

Beware of Greeks bearing gifts. ① You should be suspicious of the people who are kind to you all of a sudden.

Birds of a feather flock together. ① People with similar characters or personalities often spend time together.

Blood is thicker than water. ① Relationships with family members are the strongest and are stronger than the relationships with other people.

Blood will out. ① Someone's personal character, which is determined by the condition of their birth, will be eventually and inevitably revealed.

C

Charity begins at home. ① A person's first responsibility is to assist and take care of their own family and friends.

Children and fools tell the truth. ① Neither the children nor the fools are aware of the fact that it is sometimes in their interests to lie.

Cleanliness is next to godliness. ① A clean body is just as significant as a pure soul.

Clear moon, frost soon. ① When the sky at night is clear, the surface of the earth will cool rapidly.

Clothes don't make the man. ① You cannot judge a person only by their external appearances.

Constant occupation prevents temptation. ① If you are on the job all the time, you tend to resist the temptation.

D

Dead men tell no lies. ① People who are dead cannot tell secrets.

Death is the great leveller. ① Death applies to everyone on equal terms, because it does not spare anyone, not even the wealthy, famous, or talented.

Diamonds cut diamonds. ① It is a situation in which two equally cunning or devious people spar or interact.

Diligence is the mother of good fortune. ① If you work hard and carefully, you will be far more likely to succeed as if luck had come your way.

Discretion is the better part of valour. ① It is better to avoid a risky or dangerous situation.

Diseases of the soul are more dangerous than those of the body. ① Emotional or mental suffering is more severe than bodily pain. It has the potential to make people insane and do things that they never normally do.

Distance makes the heart grow fonder. ① When you are away from the person you love, you will have more affection for them.

Dogs of the same street bark alike. ① People whose backgrounds are identical will have identical behaviour.

Don't bark if you can't bite. ① One must not make a promise if one cannot keep one's word.

Don't count your chickens before they're hatched. ① You must not be too confident that something will succeed.

Don't dig your grave with our own knife and fork. ① Don't do something that brings about or leads to your own downfall.

Don't judge a book by its cover. ① Don't judge someone or something by looking at their appearances.

E

Early to bed, and early to rise, makes a man healthy, wealthy and wise. ① Going to bed and waking up early will make a contribution towards a person's health and success.

Elbow grease is the best polish. ① Well begun is half done but without hard work, there will not be a good outcome.

Empty vessels make the most noise. ① The people with the least talent and knowledge usually speak the loudest and create the most fuss.

Every ass likes to hear himself bray. ① Foolish people appear to be fond of their own ugly voices, since they are talkative.

Every man for himself. ① You must consider your own interests before those of others.

Every man has his price. ① Everyone is open to bribery in some way with respect to giving opinions or providing support.

Every man is the architect of his own fortune. ① The failure or success in life of each person is controlled or influenced by how they behave.

Every path has its puddle. ① Progress is rarely without occasional troubled times.

Every rose has its thorn. ① Every good thing has something unpleasant about it.

Every why has a wherefore. ① There is a 'why' for everything.

Everything in the garden is rosy. ① Everything is fine.

Experience is the father of wisdom. ① Experiencing different things will enable you to gain most wisdom and have better judgement.

F

Facts speak louder than words. ① People's actions show what they are really like rather than what they say.

Failure teaches success. ① People can learn from their past failures or mistakes and can succeed later on.

Fair exchange is no robbery. ① Swapping two items of equivalent value is an honest deal.

False friends are worse than open enemies. ① It is better to know who your real enemies are rather than blindly trusting someone who may stab you in the back.

Familiarity breeds contempt. ① Having extensive knowledge of someone often leads to loss of respect for them.

Finders keepers, losers weepers. ① It is said by a child, who has found an object and has no intention of giving it back, to another child who has lost it.

Fine words butter no parsnips. ① You can achieve success by action and nothing is achieved by empty promises or flattery.

First come, first served. ① The first one in the queue will be served first.

Fool me once, shame on you; fool me twice, shame on me. ① After being deceived once, one should learn from one's mistakes and avoid being deceived likewise again.

Fools rush in where angels fear to tread. ① People without any experience or judgement become involved in situations that the wisest would avoid.

Friendship is like money, easier made than kept. ① It is easy to befriend someone when you first meet them but it takes great effort to maintain a friendship with them.

Friendship is love with understanding. ① In friendships, you love a person with a complete knowledge of their good and bad side. However, the feelings of love in a romantic relationship will often make you "blind" to the bad side of your lover.

G

Gardens are not made by sitting in the shade. ① You cannot achieve anything without making an effort.

Give someone an inch and they will take a mile. ① If you make concession to someone, they will want more from you and they will never satisfy.

Give someone an inch and they will take a yard. ① If you make concession to someone, they will want more from you and they will never satisfy.

Give someone enough rope and they will hang themselves. ① If you give someone enough time and freedom, this will spell trouble for them.

God helps those who help themselves. ① Success comes to those who work hard to achieve it.

Good accounting makes good friends. ① You will maintain good friendship with your friends if you can avoid arguments over money.

Good and quickly seldom meet. ① A job done well takes time.

Good management is better than good income. ① Income can be lost if it is used in a careless manner or unwisely.

Grasp all, lose all. ① Endeavouring to obtain everything will often end in gaining nothing.

Great minds think alike. ① Smart and intelligent people very often have the same opinion or idea simultaneously.

Great oaks grow from small acorns. ① Good things may stem from small and insignificant beginnings.

Grief divided is made lighter. ① If you show your sorrow, it will be less painful to bear.

H

Half a loaf is better than none. ① Even if something is not as much as you wanted, you must be grateful for what you already have.

Handsome is as handsome does. ① The behaviour and the character of a person are more important than the appearance of a person.

Hard words break no bones. ① Although hearing criticism or suffering from verbal attacks may not be pleasant to you, these verbal attacks will not harm you physically.

Haste makes waste. ① If you attempt to do something quickly without proper planning, you are prone to make mistakes, and you often end up completing it more slowly.

Hatred is as blind as love. ① A person who hates others does not see any qualities in the person whom they hate.

He can who believes he can. ① You will be able to accomplish something if you believe in yourself.

He has enough who is content. ① A happy person does not need more than they already have.

He who hesitates is lost. ① A good opportunity could be lost if one were to delay a decision for too long.

He who is everywhere is nowhere. ① It is a bad idea to do too many things at the same time.

He who know nothing doubts nothing. ① We only make choices because we have knowledge.

He who laughs last, laughs best. ① Never express your triumph or joy too soon because you do not know the outcome of something until the very end.

He who pays the piper calls the tune. ① The one providing the money for something should be the one deciding on how it is spent.

He who plays with fire gets burnt. ① You are likely to run into problems if you choose to behave in a risky way.

He who wills the end wills the means. ① When you have the determination, you will find a suitable method to do something.

Health is better than wealth. ① It is better to be in fine fettle than to be rich.

Home is where the heart is. ① A place is considered home to you if you know that people you love are in that place.

Honesty is the best policy. ① It is always better to be honest.

Honey catches more flies than vinegar. ① You have to be nice to others if you want them to cooperate with you.

However long the night, the dawn will break. ① Bad things do not continue indefinitely.

Hunger is a good sauce. ① All food will taste good to you when you are hungry.

I

If a camel gets his nose in a tent, his body will follow. ① Your life will be difficult if you let something intrusive enter your life.

If in February there be no rain, it is neither good for hay nor grain. ① Grains and plants will not grow well should there be no rain in early Spring.

If two ride a horse, one must ride behind. ① When two persons are doing something together, one person can only be a leader while the other person will become the subordinate of the leader.

If wishes were horses, then beggars would ride. ① It is useless wishing alone that something will happen or come true without doing anything to make it happen or come true.

If you are patient in one moment of anger, you will avoid 100 days of sorrow. ① Taking the time to think before acting or speaking angrily will avoid you from regretting later on.

If you chase two rabbits, you will not catch either one. ① If you attempt to do two things simultaneously, you will end up not accomplishing either of them.

If you want a friend, be a friend. ① For friends to exist, both parties must make it happen.

Ignorance is bliss. ① One will not feel worried or sad when one does not know about something.

In for a penny, in for a pound. ① It is better to spend the money or time required for something to be completed once you have started to do it.

In the land of the blind the one-eyed man is king. ① A person whose ability is limited has an advantage over a person who is less able.

In times of prosperity friends are plentiful. ① You will have a great deal of friends when you are not in time of difficulties.

It is always darkest before the dawn. ① Things often seem at their worst just before they get better.

It never rains but it pours. ① A situation will worsen when one bad thing happens followed by a series of bad things.

It takes all sorts to make a world. ① It is a good thing that people vary in their abilities and character.

It's no use crying over spilt milk. ① It is pointless regretting over something that has happened and cannot be remedied.

J

Justice delayed is justice denied. ① Justice will become non-existent should the law be applied too late.

K

Kill not the goose that lays the golden egg. ① You should not destroy the source of your good fortune.

Kindle not a fire you cannot put out. ① Do not begin doing something that you can neither control nor resolve.

Kindness begets kindness. ① People will be kind to you if you are kind to them initially.

Knowledge in youth is wisdom in age. ① What you learned when you were young is valuable to you when you gradually become old.

Knowledge is power. ① Without knowledge, no great work can be done because knowledge not only will enable people to achieve success but also is more powerful than physical strength.

L

Laughter is the best medicine. ① What makes people feel good is their laughter.

Learn to walk before you run. ① Never rush into doing something if you do not know how to do it.

Learning is a treasure that will follow its owner everywhere. ① What you can keep forever is your education.

Least said, soonest mended. ① An incident is more easily forgotten provided that you talk less about it.

Let bygones be bygones. ① Forget our past quarrels and let us forgive each other.

Let the chips fall where they may. ① We should not attempt to control our destiny given that it is often not within our reach.

Liars need good memories. ① Liars must be careful when it comes to remember what they say.

Lightning never strikes in the same place twice. ① It is unlikely that an unusual event would happen again if one were in the same circumstances as before.

Like father, like son. ① A son's character can be expected to be like that of his father.

Little strokes fell good oaks. ① It is easier to do a task when you divide it into smaller parts.

Look before you leap. ① Never take a course of action without considering the possible consequences.

Loose lips sink ships. ① Large losses are the cost of disclosing important information to a competitor or an enemy.

Love is blind. ① A person who falls in love does not see the faults of their lover.

M

Make a silk purse out of a sow's ear. ① Make something good using poor materials.

Man proposes, God disposes. ① A person can make plans but whether or not they are successful hinges on God's will.

Manners make the man. ① A person is judged by their conduct and manners.

Many a true word is spoken in jest. ① Some humorous remarks can contain either true or serious statements.

Many hands make light work. ① A task is easier to accomplish if the work relating to it is shared amongst others.

Mark, learn and inwardly digest. ① To assimilate something thoroughly involves noting and reflecting upon it.

Marry in haste, repent at leisure. ① If you do not know someone well enough and marry them later, you will end up regretting about it.

Memory is the treasure of the mind. ① Having a good memory is something considered as very precious.

Men make houses, women make homes. ① The men build or acquire houses for their family while the women turn the houses into homes.

Might as well be hanged for a sheep as for a lamb. ① You might as well commit a greater offence should the penalty be the same for committing a smaller offence.

Misery loves company. ① People who are feeling sad like to share their troubles with others.

Money begets money. ① You can make more money out of the money that you already have.

Money doesn't grow on trees. ① You need to be careful not to waste money because it is not easily obtained or plentiful.

More haste, less speed. ① If you attempt to do something quickly without proper planning, you are prone to make mistakes, and you often end up completing it more slowly.

N

Necessity is the mother of invention. ① When there is the need to do something, you will eventually think of a way to do it.

Need teaches a plan. ① The need for something will force you to find a solution for it.

Needs must when the devil drives. ① Sometimes you are forced to do something you would rather not do.

Neither a borrower nor a lender be. ① You should not lend or borrow money from a friend because in so doing, you will lose your friend and your money.

Never put off till tomorrow what can be done today. ① Do not postpone doing something later when you can do it now.

Never say die. ① This is said to encourage someone to keep trying.

Never trouble trouble until trouble troubles you. ① Do not ask for trouble in advance and only deal with the trouble when it is necessary to do so or when it arises. ② Do not worry about something before it has happened.

No man can serve two masters. ① It is not possible to take orders from two superiors.

No man is a hero to his valet. ① A close personal servant can see all his master's failings.

No man is an island. ① Everyone relies on others, and no one is self-sufficient.

No news is good news. ① You can assume that all is well without information to the contrary.

No pain, no gain. ① You cannot achieve anything without putting in the effort.

No rain, no grain. ① The harvest will be poor without rain.

No smoke without fire. ① There are always some reasons for a rumour or some truth in a rumour.

No wind, no waves. ① There are always some reasons for a rumour or some truth in a rumour.

Nobody is perfect. ① People occasionally make mistakes.

Nothing ventured nothing gained. ① Do not expect to achieve anything if you are not prepared to take any risk.

O

Once bitten, twice shy. ① People are more careful to avoid the same thing from happening again after they have undergone a bad experience.

One father is worth more than a hundred schoolmasters. ① No teacher can replace a father.

One good turn deserves another. ① You should take the chance to repay a favour to someone who has done you a favour.

One man's meat is another man's poison. ① People do not always have the same liking for a certain thing.

One man's trash is another man's treasure. ① What is considered as useless to one person could be considered as valuable to another person.

One of these days is none of these days. ① A promise is vague unless someone sets a date on when they will fulfil this promise.

One swallow doesn't make a summer. ① A single fortunate or satisfactory event does not mean that all the other events following it will be also good.

One today is worth two tomorrows. ① What you have today is better than what is hoped for or promised.

Only real friends will tell you when your face is dirty. ① Only a true friend will tell you the truth.

Opportunity seldom knocks twice. ① Take the opportunity whenever it arises because it may not come again.

Out of sight, out of mind. ① We have a tendency to forget the things or people that we do not see.

Out of the mouth of babes and sucklings. ① Wisdom often comes out from the mouths of the children.

P

Penny wise, pound foolish. ① The proverb is used for describing a person who is careful about spending small sum of money, but careless about spending a large sum of money.

People who live in glass houses should not throw stones. ① One should not criticise other people for weaknesses in their characters that one also has oneself.

Pity is akin to love. ① You may start to love someone if you begin to feel sorry for them.

Poverty waits at the gates of idleness. ① You will not earn any money if you do not work.

Practice makes perfect. ① The only way to become good at something is to do it repeatedly.

Prevention is better than cure. ① It is easier for one to prevent something from happening than to cure the disease or to repair the damage later.

Pride comes before a fall. ① Do not be too confident about your abilities because you will look foolish when something bad happens.

Procrastination is the thief of time. ① An action that is delayed for too long is simply a waste of time.

Punctuality is the soul of business. ① You should always be punctual for your business appointments.

R

Revenge is sweet. ① There is a feeling of satisfaction from harming someone who has harmed you before.

Rome was not built in a day. ① You must take the time to do a job properly and you cannot expect to have it done quickly.

Save me from my friends. ① Our friends are sometimes more dangerous than our enemies.

Saying is one thing, doing is another. ① People do not always do what they have promised to do.

Short reckonings make long friends. ① Money borrowed from friends should be repaid as soon as possible to maintain healthy friendships.

Sickness in the body brings sadness to the mind. ① The cause of depression or sadness is due to physical suffering.

Silence gives consent. ① You are assumed to agree with something to which you do not object verbally.

Snug as a bug in a rug. ① It is a proverb for describing a person who is in a very comfortable situation or position.

Spare the rod and spoil the child. ① The personal development of the children will suffer if they are not punished when they do wrong.

Speech is silver, silence is golden. ① Discretion can be better or more valuable than speaking the most eloquent words.

Sticks and stones will break my bones but names will never hurt me. ① Physical attacks may harm me, but verbal attacks do not.

Still waters run deep. ① Although a person does not say a lot, they may possess a great deal of knowledge or wisdom.

Stolen fruit is sweet. ① The most tempting things are the forbidden ones.

Stolen pleasures are the sweetest. ① The most tempting things are the forbidden ones.

Tall oaks grow from little acorns. ① Small beginnings may be the start of many great things to come.

The apple doesn't fall far from the tree. ① Children look and behave like their parents.

The best advice is found on the pillow. ① If we have a problem, we may find the solution after a good night's sleep.

The best helping hand is at the end of your sleeve. ① Doing something by yourself is the best way to getting it done.

The best things in life are free. ① You should give priority to free and important things like family and friends, happiness, and good health over those things that cost money.

The darkest hour is just before dawn. ① Things often seem at their worst just before they get better.

The devil looks after his own. ① Success or good fortune always seems to come to those who least deserve it.

The devil makes work for idle hands. ① People who are idle or out of work will often become troublemakers.

The die is cast. ① It is not possible to change a decision that has been made.

The early bird catches the worm. ① One wanting to be more successful than others or having an advantage over others must act early or act before them.

The end justifies the means. ① Unfair or wrong methods could be employed if it leads to good result or a desired outcome when one is carrying out this action.

The first step is the hardest. ① The commencement of an action is the most difficult part of all.

The more you have, the more you want. ① People have a greedy mind to possess more and more.

The mouse that has but one hole is quickly taken. ① You are left with no alternatives if you meet with failure and if you are dependent on only one course of action.

The pen is mightier than the sword. ① Communication and words are more effective than fighting and war.

The proof of the pudding is in the eating. ① We can only judge the real value of something if it has been tested or tried.

The road to hell is paved with good intentions. ① Having an intention to do something is not good enough if one does not do it at the end.

The tongue wounds more than a lance. ① Having physical injuries is less harmful than having been insulted.

The truth is in the wine. ① A person is more likely to speak honestly when they are drunk due to the effects of alcohol consumption.

The way to a man's heart is though his stomach. ① A man will love you when you feed him well.

The wish is father to the thought. ① Something that you think is true is simply because you want it to be true.

There is a black sheep in every flock. ① There is always someone who neither perform nor behave like the others.

There is a trick in every trade. ① It is the norm to follow the traditional ways of doing things.

There is no fool like an old fool. ① It is expected of an older person to behave more sensibly.

There is safety in numbers. ① A person will feel more confident when they are in a crowd.

There's many a slip between the cup and the lip. ① Only when we actually get something, then it is possible to say that we have ownership of it.

Time and tide wait for no man. ① Events will happen regardless whether one delays a decision or not.

Time has wings. ① Time passes by quickly.

Time heals all wounds. ① The impact of the bad events on someone will lessen as time goes by.

Time is money. ① Time cannot afford to be wasted.

To err is human, to forgive divine. ① It is natural for people to make mistakes, and therefore it is important to forgive people when they do.

Too many cooks spoil the broth. ① Things cannot be done properly if there are too many people involved in doing them at the same time.

Too much bed makes a dull head. ① One does not have a clear head when one is sleeping excessively.

Trust not a horse's heel nor a dog's tooth. ① A horse kicks from behind while a dog attacks with teeth.

Truth has no answer. ① It is not possible for one to refute what is true or to argue against the facts.

Truth is stranger than fiction. ① Events in fiction are often not as strange as what actually occurs in life.

Two wrongs don't make a right. ① Just because someone has harmed you does not mean that it is correct for you to harm them in return.

Union is strength. ① The combined force of a group is more than that of an individual.

Unwillingness easily finds an excuse. ① A person will always find a reason to avoid doing something that they don't want to do.

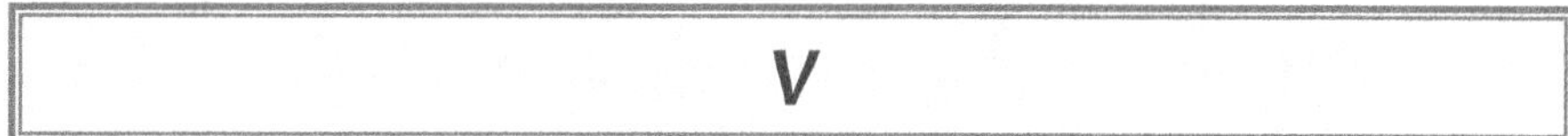

Variety is the spice of life. ① Life is made more interesting by doing many different things.

Virtue is its own reward. ① One acting in a correct or moral way should not expect to receive praise from others because one is expected to do.

Walls have ears. ① People could be listening to what you are saying so you must be careful where you talk.

Waste not, want not. ① Never waste anything that does not serve your purpose.

What a man says drunk, he thinks sober. ① People who are under the influence of alcohol honestly will speak more.

What soberness conceals, drunkenness reveals. ① People who are under the influence of alcohol are less discreet.

What the eye doesn't see, the heart doesn't grieve over. ① Nothing can hurt a person if they do not know about something.

When in Rome, do as the Romans do. ① The one who is visiting a country or its people should adopt their customs as shown by one's behaviour.

When poverty comes in the door, love goes out the window. ①
A couple's relationship becomes problematic when the couple lose
everything.

When the cat's away, the mice play. ① When the person in
authority is absent, people will generally misbehave.

Where there's a will there's a way. ① A solution to a problem can
only be found if there is a determination to do it.

Where there's life there's hope. ① Provided that a person is still
breathing, there is some hope for their recovery.

Who makes himself a sheep will be eaten by the wolves. ①
Anyone can be misled if they are easily influenced by others.

Wisdom is better than strength. ① Using your own intelligence is
more preferable to using your own physical strength.

Wonders will never cease! ① It is used humorously for saying that
you feel very surprised and happy about something.

Worry often gives a small thing a big shadow. ① To worry over
small details makes the problem of something seem worse than it
should be.

Y

You are never too old to learn. ① Age does not matter when one
is always learning something new.

You are what you eat. ① Whatever you eat will have an impact on
your health.

You can lead a horse to water but you can't make it drink. ①
You can at best offer somebody a chance to do something but you
cannot force them to do it.

You can't teach an old dog new tricks. ① A person who sticks to
their old way of doing things will not change their way of doing things.

You never know what you can do until you try. ① Do have an
attempt to do something before making a decision not to do it.

You scratch my back and I'll scratch yours. ① I will help you if
you help me.